"The biblical offices of prophet, priest, categories to make sense of Christ's per: fore grateful for this new volume by Ri(the reader through each of these three anointed offices in the Old Testament, and provides some ways that they illumine the work of Christ as the One who was anointed with the Holy Spirit beyond measure. This is a fine introduction not only to prophet, priest, and king in the Old Testament, but also to the person and work of Christ in the New."
— **Brandon D. Crowe**, Associate Professor of New Testament, Westminster Theological Seminary

"Although Reformed theologians have long recognized the importance of the three offices of Christ, there have been few sustained works on this essential topic in the last few generations. Thankfully, Dick Belcher has stepped forward to fill this gap in biblical scholarship. With wisdom, clarity, and grace, Belcher guides the reader to a richer and fuller vision of Christ as Prophet, Priest, and King."
— **Michael J. Kruger**, President and Samuel C. Patterson Professor of New Testament, Reformed Theological Seminary, Charlotte, North Carolina

"It is common today for Christians to speak of Christ as the fulfillment of all that the Scriptures teach. Richard Belcher has shown how this is true by focusing on the developments of prophetic, priestly, and royal themes in the Bible. As delightful as this is, he has gone further. Rather than simply speaking of Christ as the fulfillment of these themes, he has also drawn out the practical implications of prophetic, priestly, and royal service for all who follow Christ. Belcher's work points us all toward the importance of keeping the centrality of Christ in view as we address the manifold challenges that Christians face as we long for his return in glory."
— **Richard L. Pratt Jr.**, President, Third Millennium Ministries

"The Reformation viewed the threefold office of prophet, priest, and king (munus triplex) as fundamentally important to the understanding of Christ's work in redemption, and Dr. Belcher's impressive treatment of these offices in their biblical-theological setting is essential reading in understanding their comprehensive nature. This book deftly combines biblical and pastoral insight that is most welcome in furthering our understanding of Scripture and the person and work of Christ. Enthusiastically recommended."

—**Derek W. H. Thomas**, Senior Minister, First Presbyterian Church, Columbia, South Carolina; Robert Strong Professor of Systematic and Pastoral Theology, Reformed Theological Seminary, Atlanta, Georgia

PROPHET, PRIEST, AND KING

THE ROLES OF CHRIST IN THE BIBLE AND OUR ROLES TODAY

RICHARD P. BELCHER JR.

P U B L I S H I N G

P.O. BOX 817 • PHILLIPSBURG • NEW JERSEY 08865-0817

Printed in the United States of America

ISBN: 978-1-59638-502-3 (pbk)
ISBN: 978-1-62995-192-8 (ePub)
ISBN: 978-1-62995-193-5 (Mobi)

Library of Congress Cataloging-in-Publication Data

Names: Belcher, Richard P., Jr., author.
Title: Prophet, priest, and king : the roles of Christ in the Bible and our roles today / Richard P. Belcher Jr.
Description: Phillipsburg : P&R Publishing, 2016. | Includes bibliographical references and index.
Identifiers: LCCN 2016017047| ISBN 9781596385023 (pbk.) | ISBN 9781629951928 (epub) | ISBN 9781629951935 (mobi)
Subjects: LCSH: Jesus Christ--Person and offices. | Typology (Theology)
Classification: LCC BT203 .B4467 2016 | DDC 232--dc23
LC record available at https://lccn.loc.gov/2016017047

To Michael Dixon and Chris Sewell
Sons-in-law
Brothers in Christ
Fellow Participants in Ministry

CONTENTS

Analytical Outline

33

7. Christ as King in His Humiliation and Exaltation
    A. Jesus as King during His Earthly Ministry
        (1) Dominion over Creation
        (2) Dominion over the Demons
        (3) The Kingdom of God
            a. Jewish Expectations of the Kingdom
            b. The Present Reality of the Kingdom
            c. The Spiritual Nature of the Kingdom
            d. The Future Glory of the Kingdom
        (4) The Suffering of the King
    B. Jesus as King in Ruling at the Right Hand of the Father

8. Prophet, Priest, and King: Implications for the Church
    A. The Prophetic Ministry of the Church
        (1) Joel's Prophecy and the Day of Pentecost
        (2) Word and Worship
        (3) The Prophetic Role of Elders
        (4) Implications of Prophet, Priest, and King for Preaching
        (5) The Prophetic Role of Individual Believers
    B. The Priestly Ministry of the Church
        (1) The "Service" of the Levites
        (2) The Priestly Ministry of Elders in Worship
        (3) The Priestly Role of Individual Believers
    C. The Kingly Ministry of the Church
        (1) The Rule of Elders
        (2) The Dominion of Individual Believers
    D. Conclusion

FOREWORD

IN *PROPHET, PRIEST, AND KING: A Biblical Theology of the Offices of Christ*, Richard "Dick" Belcher takes his readers on a super-elevated rail through a well-worn track. The theme of prophet, priest, and king has been treated in numerous systematic theologies. But now all the freshness of new insights from a biblical-theological approach stimulates the reader's mind and soul. Rather than rehearsing the all-important work of systematic theologians on these significant topics, Belcher begins at the beginning of scriptural testimony regarding the three offices, traces their development through various old covenant phases, and climaxes with new covenant consummations.

As you travel the track of ever-enriching developments of prophet, priest, and king from biblical beginnings through prophets and psalms into new covenant climaxes, expect to learn deepening truths all along the way. Belcher focuses on the correct texts, illuminates them with insightful analyses, and draws out correct conclusions. The three offices are united in Adam and Abraham. But sin disrupts, and the offices remain divided in Israel, though their functions are sometimes shared.

The prediction of a coming Prophet like Moses (Deut. 18:15, 18) anticipates both the plurality of prophets and the singularity of One who is uniquely like Moses. The role of these prophets in occasionally anointing kings indicates that the ruler must govern according to God's Word. The ministry of prayer must not be overlooked. Jesus Christ proved himself to be the Prophet like Moses by his display of might in word, prayer, suffering, and deed. The ongoing role of the prophet's function in the church today comes to expression principally in the elder who preaches the Word.

Be prepared to learn many things about the old covenant priest, his anointing, his clothing, and his often-overlooked role as teacher of the Word. Jesus was not identified as Priest while on earth, since he was of the order of Melchizedek. Yet his purifying action of cleansing the temple disclosed his identity as High Priest over God's house.

In treating the topic of kingship, Belcher displays full awareness of the latest research in the structure of the Psalter. The phrases concluding Book 4 in Psalm 106 find their corresponding response in the opening phrases of Book 5 in Psalm 107. The question of a "royal priesthood" leads Belcher to a sane evaluation of the question whether David himself functions as priest as well as king in the line of Melchizedek (Ps. 110:4). The Christology of Colossians 1:15 that describes Jesus Christ as the "firstborn" of all creation finds its proper framework for interpretation in Psalm 89:27, which designates David as the "firstborn, the highest of the kings of the earth."

In a day in which narrow specialization torments biblical research, Belcher proves himself capable of dealing with both the technical subtleties and the broader sweeps of biblical theology. Widely read in both old covenant and new covenant literature, Belcher never loses his reader in the morass of unending interactions among contemporary scholars. Instead, he stays close to the heart of the subject, enlightening his reader all along the way. As a consequence, he has made a significant contribution to the church's understanding of the breadth and length and depth and height of Scripture's teaching on the important subjects of prophet, priest, and king.

O. Palmer Robertson
Director, African Bible University of Uganda

Acknowledgments

I BECAME INTERESTED in the topic *Prophet, Priest, and King* when I began to think through how the Psalms relate to Christ. Considering his various roles opened up avenues for reflecting on the many ways in which the Psalms and other Old Testament passages could connect to Christ. It became apparent that no one book covered all three roles in their Old Testament context and in their relationship to Christ. This book will have a chapter on each role in the Old Testament and a chapter on how Christ fulfills each role in the New Testament. There is also a chapter on the implications of these roles for the church. Study questions at the end of each chapter facilitate discussion for the use of this book in Bible studies.

Many people have assisted and encouraged me in this book's completion. I would like to thank Dr. Robert Peterson for his interest in this topic and his help in talking through the project. I am grateful to P&R Publishing for its assistance in publishing. I am very thankful to Dr. Ligon Duncan, the Chancellor of Reformed Theological Seminary (RTS), and to the board of RTS for their commitment to scholarship and for the sabbatical granted to me to finish this book. I am blessed to teach at the Charlotte campus, and I thank Dr. Michael J. Kruger for his continuing encouragement to pursue this topic and to complete this book.

Many others have given essential help without which this book would not have been written. I would like to thank my teaching assistant, Zachary Keuthan, who tracked down many sources that I needed and helped in editing the manuscript. I would also like to thank his wife, Elly, who works in the library at RTS Charlotte, for her prompt help in requesting books and articles that were needed. I would like to thank Kim Macurda, the registrar at RTS Charlotte, for her competent work that allows me to be Academic Dean and to teach and write as much as I do. I would also like to thank my family for making life so enjoyable, and for my wife, Lu, who faithfully does so many things.

This book is dedicated to Michael Dixon and Chris Sewell. It is a blessing to have two sons-in-law who love the Lord, but it is also a great joy that both of them are ordained ministers of the gospel.

Richard P. Belcher Jr.
August 2015

Abbreviations

ANE	Ancient Near East
BSac	*Bibliotheca Sacra*
ESV	English Standard Version
JBL	*Journal of Biblical Literature*
JETS	*Journal of the Evangelical Theological Society*
NASB	New American Standard Bible
NIDOTTE	Willem A. VanGemeren, ed., *New International Dictionary of Old Testament Theology and Exegesis* (Grand Rapids: Zondervan, 1997)
NIV	New International Version
NKJV	New King James Version
NT	New Testament
OT	Old Testament
TWOT	R. Laird Harris, et al., *Theological Wordbook of the Old Testament* (Chicago: Moody Press, 1980)
TynBul	*Tyndale Bulletin*
UT	Urim and Thummim
WCF	Westminster Confession of Faith
WLC	Westminster Larger Catechism
WSC	Westminster Shorter Catechism
WTJ	*Westminster Theological Journal*
ZAW	*Zeitschrift für die alttestamentliche Wissenschaft*

I

The Importance of
Prophet, Priest, and King

MANY CHRISTIANS TEND to think of Christ's work as one-dimensional. Sometimes only the priestly role is emphasized, or the kingship of Christ in his exaltation. Many times Christ's prophetic role is neglected, or his role as King in his humiliation. This can lead to a one-sided view of Christ and his work. A well-rounded view not only understands his work in light of being Prophet, Priest, and King, but also recognizes that these offices need to be seen in light of both his humiliation and his exaltation. Christians also tend to recognize the priestly role of believers, but lack teaching on the significance of the prophet and king roles for the corporate church, her leaders, and individual believers. This book will address the work of Christ in light of the roles of Prophet, Priest, and King and will then draw out implications for the church.

Historically, the Reformed faith has emphasized the roles of Prophet, Priest, and King to discuss the work of Christ. Louis Berkhof notes that although the early church fathers speak of the different offices of Christ, Calvin first recognized the importance of distinguishing them and called attention to them in separate sections of the *Institutes of the Christian Religion* (book 2, chapter 15).[1] Others have done the same.[2] The Heidelberg Catechism also uses these roles to speak of the life of the Christian (Questions 31–32). A redemptive-historical approach—emphasizing Christ's fulfillment of the Old Testament—naturally lends itself to connecting with the roles, not just for Christ but also for his body, the church. This approach also has implications for preaching Christ from the Old Testament.

The roles of prophet, priest, and king are defined and developed as offices within the nation of Israel. But these roles are mentioned before Israel's establishment. In fact, Abraham himself is presented as fulfilling them. A brief review of the evidence will show the importance of these roles before Sinai, will lead to a partial understanding of their meaning, and will raise the question of their origin.

Prophet, Priest, and King before Israel

Abraham is called a prophet in Genesis 20, which is the first time that the word for *prophet* (*navi*, נביא) is used in Scripture. Abraham and Sarah have gone down to Gerar, and for the second time Abraham lies about his relationship to Sarah to protect his own life (see also ch. 12). King Abimelech takes Sarah into his own household, but before he can touch her, God appears to

1. Louis Berkhof, *Systematic Theology* (Grand Rapids: Eerdmans, 1941), 356–57. One early church father who made use of these categories is Eusebius. "The Church History," in *Nicene and Post-Nicene Fathers of the Christian Church*, ed. Philip Schaff and Henry Wace (Grand Rapids: Eerdmans, 1991), 1:86. The threefold office was important for Calvin as a way for faith to find a firm basis for salvation and thus to rest in Christ. David J. Englesma, *The Reformed Faith of John Calvin* (Jenison, MI: Reformed Free Publishing Association, 2009), 169–70. Berkhof comments that modern theology is averse to the offices because it is so in love with Christ as the ideal man, the loving helper, and the elder brother. Modern theology seems to fear that an emphasis on Christ as Mediator would dehumanize him.

2. Systematic theologies that use *Prophet*, *Priest*, and *King* to discuss the work of Christ include Robert Dabney, Charles Hodge, Herman Hoeksema, James Boice, Wayne

him in a dream. God warns him to return Sarah to Abraham or else face death for himself and his household, specifically telling him: "Now then, return the man's wife, for he is a prophet, so that he will pray for you, and you shall live" (20:7).

Several things in Abraham's life support this designation of prophet. In Genesis 12 he received a call from God, promising blessing to his family and all the families of the earth. In chapter 15 the word of the Lord came to Abraham in a vision. The phrase "the word of the Lord came to" is standard for describing prophetic revelation (Hos. 1:1; Joel 1:1; Jonah 1:1; Mic. 1:1), and God spoke to prophets regularly in visions (Num. 12:6; Obad. 1; Nah. 1:1; and Hab. 1:1; Amos 1:1 uses the verb "to see"). God's interaction with Abraham in Genesis 18 portrays Abraham as an intercessory prophet as he pleads for God to withhold judgment because of the number of righteous within the city. God's deliberation concerning whether to include Abraham reminds one of the divine council (Job 1:6; Ps. 89:7) and being brought into the prophetic circle (1 Kings 22:14–28; Amos 3:7).[3] The aspect of prayer in connection with being a prophet is specifically mentioned in Genesis 20. In fact, Abraham's intercession can save Abimelech because Abraham is a prophet, which assumes a close relationship with God (as demonstrated in ch. 18). Prayer will become a part of the prophet's role later in Scripture through Moses (Ex. 8; Num. 12; Deut. 32), Samuel (1 Sam. 12:23), and Jeremiah (Jer. 7:16; 11:14; 14:11–12; 18:18–20). The role of the prophet is closely connected with the word of God and prayer.

Grudem, John Frame, and Michael Horton. Significant Puritans who use *Prophet, Priest, and King* include John Owen, John Flavel, Thomas Boston, and Thomas Goodwin. See also Robert Letham, *The Work of Christ* (Downers Grove, IL: InterVarsity Press, 1993); Robert Sherman, *King, Priest, and Prophet: A Trinitarian Theology of Atonement* (New York: T&T Clark, 2004). Geoffrey Wainwright shows that Lutherans did not continue to use *Prophet, Priest,* and *King,* but that Roman Catholics and Methodists have used the terms to explain the work of Christ. *For Our Salvation: Two Approaches to the Work of Christ* (Grand Rapids: Eerdmans, 1997), 103–8.

3. Kenneth A. Mathews, *Genesis 11:27–50:26* (Nashville: Broadman & Holman, 2005), 216, 222.

Abraham also acts as a priest in building altars when he travels throughout the land of Canaan (Gen. 12). The first altar is built at Shechem in response to God's appearance and the affirmation of God's promise of descendants who will possess the land. Abraham builds another altar near Bethel, where he worships by calling on the name of the Lord. These altars are connected with the presence of God and could be how Abraham claimed the land as his response of faith in God's promise: one day the whole land will be the place of God's presence. Altars are also connected to worship and sacrifice, which highlights the priestly role.[4]

Other examples of the priestly role before Sinai are Noah and Job. After the flood, Noah builds an altar to the Lord and sacrifices burnt offerings. God responds to this act of worship by establishing his covenant with Noah. The story of Job reflects the patriarchal period and occurs outside the boundaries of Israel.[5] Job functioned as a priest to his family by offering burnt offerings on behalf of each of his children in case they had sinned against God (Job 1:5). Job performed this function in his role as their father and head of the family, with the goal to "consecrate" them. The burnt offerings would restore their relationship with God and bring them into a state of holiness fit for service to God.[6] Part of the role of the priests will be to offer sacrifices on behalf of the Israelites to bring them into a state of holiness, ensuring that God's presence will remain in their midst.

Abraham also fulfills the role of a king in defeating a coalition of armies and rescuing Lot in Genesis 14. It becomes clear that he not only is very wealthy, but also has a powerful household. Lot and Abraham separate because their possessions are so great that the

4. Although some deny the connection between altars and sacrifice because sacrifices are not specifically mentioned in the text (Cassuto, Westermann), Gordon J. Wenham points out that altars and offering sacrifices on them are integral to the worship of God. *Genesis 1–15* (Waco, TX: Word Books, 1987), 322.

5. John E. Hartley, *The Book of Job* (Grand Rapids: Eerdmans, 1988), 66.

6. Gerald H. Wilson, *Job* (Peabody, MA: Hendrickson, 2007), 20.

land could not support them both (ch. 13). Lot chooses to move to the Jordan Valley, which was well watered but near Sodom. In chapter 14 Lot gets caught up in the battles of the day. A coalition of four kings from the area of Mesopotamia—led by Chedorlaomer—seek to reassert their control over five cities of the Dead Sea rebelling after twelve years of servitude. Lot and his family, who have moved into Sodom by this time (14:12), are captured and taken as spoils of war. When Abraham hears of Lot's capture, he leads 318 men from his household to rescue Lot (v. 14). He defeats this coalition of four kings and brings back all the possessions that they had taken. Genesis 14 reads like the account of a military campaign. Abraham's force of 318 men are "trained," a word with military connotations in second-millennium texts.[7] Defeating the coalition of kings involves military strategy, and Abraham negotiates with the king of Sodom when he returns with the spoils. Abraham acts like a king defending the land by defeating a powerful group of kings and rescuing a member of his household.

The Origins of Prophet, Priest, and King in Genesis 1–3

The appearance of the roles of prophet, priest, and king before they are developed and defined as offices within Israel raises the question of their origin and the possibility that they are part of the original function that God gave to human beings in Genesis 1–3. An examination of these early chapters shows that the role of ruling (kingship) is explicitly conferred on humanity and that at a minimum, the roles of priest and prophet are implicitly assumed to be part of Adam and Eve's life.

The Role of a King

The role of ruling and exercising dominion (kingship) is explicitly stated in Genesis 1:26–28. It is clear in Genesis 1 that

7. Mathews, *Genesis 11:27–50:26*, 147.

the creation of mankind[8] is an act by God that sets human beings apart and gives them a special place. When God creates mankind, he uses terminology that was not used in reference to any other creation. The phrase "let us make" (v. 26) is unique and refers to God's self-deliberation before creating humanity.[9] The ongoing march of creation in the pattern of "God said" and then "God created" or "God made" is interrupted with "let us make" to highlight the importance of the creation of human beings. It is also significant that only human beings are created in the image of God. Although there is a lot of discussion concerning what "the image of God" means,[10] it clearly sets human beings apart from the animals. Genesis 1 presents humanity as the crown of creation, set apart in significant ways.

The special place of human beings gives them a special role. Immediately after the statement that they are created in God's image is the assertion of their function: "And let them have dominion over the fish of the sea and over the birds of the heavens and over the livestock and over all the earth and over every creeping thing that creeps on the earth" (Gen. 1:26). Then, after the statement that God made mankind male and female, God blessed them and said to them, "Be fruitful and multiply and fill the earth and subdue it, and have dominion over the fish of the sea and over the birds of the heavens and over every living thing that moves on the earth" (v. 28).

The function of human beings within God's creation is a royal one that is patterned after the God who created them. They are to reflect the image of God. He created the world and all that is in it by his power, and human beings—being male and female—are to procreate by being fruitful, multiplying, and filling the earth.

---

8. The Hebrew word (*adam*, אדם) is used in a generic sense for humanity (Gen. 1:26).

9. This section is a summary of the discussion in Richard P. Belcher Jr., *Genesis: The Beginning of God's Plan of Salvation* (Ross-shire, UK: Christian Focus, 2012), 54–57. Discussions of the options for the meaning of "let us make" are found there.

10. See the discussion in ibid., 55.

Marriage is later instituted for humans to carry out this mandate from God (Gen. 2:24), who sets marriage apart as the appropriate place for becoming one flesh and raising children. God also gives human beings the function of ruling over creation. This rule includes dominion, which entails a governing aspect, such as in Genesis 2 when Adam names the animals, demonstrating his authority over them. This rule includes subduing creation, which has the idea of asserting control over or making something subservient to someone else's purposes. Even before the fall, subduing creation would have been appropriate in the work that God gave Adam and Eve. Dominion would have included taking the "domesticated" life in the garden, represented by plants that need human cultivation to grow (v. 5), and the world outside the garden, represented by the plants that grow on their own.[11]

The teaching of humanity's dominion is a debated issue, but dominion does not mean that human beings can exploit God's creation.[12] They can appropriately use creation for their own benefit and the benefit of others, but they carry out this role under the authority of God. Dominion is not an autonomous function letting humans do whatever they please.[13] Rather, humans pattern

11. For a discussion of the relationship between Genesis 1–2 and the view that Genesis 2:5 looks forward to the cultivated plants of the garden in distinction from the plants that grow on their own in Genesis 1, see ibid., 32–33.

12. Blaming the Christian's view of dominion for the ecological crisis goes back to a seminal article by Lynn White Jr., "The Historical Roots of Our Ecological Crisis," in an appendix to Francis Schaeffer, *Pollution and the Death of Man* (Wheaton, IL: Tyndale House, 1970), 97–116 (originally published in *Science* 155 [1967]: 1203–7). Other works that agree with this view include Norman C. Habel, ed., *The Earth Bible*, 4 vols. (Sheffield, UK: Sheffield Academic Press, 2001), and Norman C. Habel and Peter Trudinger, eds., *Exploring Ecological Hermeneutics* (Atlanta: Society of Biblical Literature, 2008). The approach in these works denies that humans are at the center of the universe and argues that (1) the universe/earth and all its components have intrinsic worth; (2) the earth is a subject capable of raising its voice in celebration and against injustice; and (3) the earth is a balanced and diverse domain where responsible custodians can function as partners—rather than rulers—to sustain a balanced and diverse community.

13. James Barr, who is not an evangelical, pointed out that the great modern exploitation of nature has taken place under the reign of liberal humanism, in which human beings no longer see themselves as under the authority of a Creator. This easily leads to

this activity after God's activity in Genesis 1–2. In chapter 1 God is presented as the sovereign Creator of the universe who rules over his creation by forming and fashioning it. Mankind's dominion imitates God's rule, so that humans carry out this function under his authority. It is interesting that in chapter 2 God is presented as personally caring for his creation when he provides for all of Adam and Eve's needs. The role of human beings in chapter 2 imitates God's role as they care for and keep the garden. Genesis 1 and 2 together present a complete picture and a proper balance of humanity's role.[14] Clearly, human beings have a royal calling of rule and dominion (kingship) within God's creation.

The Role of a Priest

The role of priest is not as explicit in Genesis 2 as the role of king is in Genesis 1, but the work that God gave Adam to do in the garden has priestly connotations.[15] The garden of Eden is a special place of God's presence that foreshadows the later tab-

---

the dominance of nature with an unlimited right to dispose of it as one sees fit. James Barr, "Man and Nature," in *Ecology and Religion in History*, ed. David Spring and Eileen Spring (New York: Harper & Row, 1974), quoted in Joseph Blenkinsopp, *Treasures Old and New: Essays in the Theology of the Pentateuch* (Grand Rapids: Eerdmans, 2004), 38. Recent works that take a mediating position between the dominion model and the stewardship model include Richard Bauckham, *The Bible and Ecology: Rediscovering the Community of Creation* (Waco, TX: Baylor, 2010), and Richard Bauckham, *Living with Other Creatures: Green Exegesis and Theology* (Waco, TX: Baylor, 2011).

14. For a perspective that seeks to treat the environment properly but also rejects global alarmist views and views focused on major government intervention, see "The Cornwall Declaration," in *Environmental Stewardship in the Judeo-Christian Tradition: Jewish, Catholic, and Protestant Wisdom on the Environment*, ed. Michael B. Barkey (Grand Rapids: Acton Institute, 2000).

15. Dan Lioy, *Axis of Glory: A Biblical and Theological Analysis of the Temple Motif in Scripture* (New York: Lang, 2010), 122. He points out that before the fall, God and human beings did not need a mediator. Adam and Eve lived in the presence of God and served in the garden. This may explain why the priestly role is implicit in Genesis 1–2. John Owen denies that there was a priestly role in the garden because the role of priests must include the offering of sacrifices. *The Priesthood of Christ: Its Necessity and Nature* (Ross-shire, UK: Christian Focus, 2010), 40–46. Although there was no need to offer sacrifices in the garden of Eden before sin, the role of priests is broader than offering sacrifices.

ernacle and temple. It is an enclosed, protected area associated with the presence and blessings of God. A river flows out of the garden, representing the abundant blessings flowing from the place of God's presence, a picture later found in Psalm 46, Ezekiel 47, and Revelation 22. Cherubim also guard the garden when Adam and Eve are expelled.[16]

The garden is not only a sanctuary for fellowship with God. The two verbs used to describe Adam's work in the garden (Gen. 2:15) are also used of the priest's work in the tabernacle (Num. 3:7–8; 8:26; 18:5–6). The verbs are to guard (shamar, שׁמר) and to serve/work (avad, אבד). Adam was placed in the garden "to work it and to keep it," and the Levites were given to the priests to assist by keeping "guard over him [Aaron] and over the whole congregation before the tent of meeting, as they minister [serve] at the tabernacle" (3:7). The Levites were also to "guard all the furnishings of the tent of meeting" (v. 8) and assist the priests in the Tent of Meeting "by keeping guard" (8:26). Although there were certain things the Levites could not do in the tabernacle (v. 26), they had oversight to ensure that it was transported correctly and that its holiness was maintained, especially in relationship

---

16. Much more could be said concerning the relationship between the garden and the later temple. See G. K. Beale, *The Temple and the Church's Mission: A Biblical Theology of the Dwelling Place of God* (Downers Grove, IL: InterVarsity Press, 2004), 66–80; Lioy, *Axis of Glory*, 5–16. For an approach that raises questions concerning whether the garden should be understood as a temple or a place of God's presence, see Daniel I. Block, "Eden: A Temple? A Reassessment of the Biblical Evidence," in *From Creation to New Creation: Biblical Theology and Exegesis*, ed. Daniel M. Gurtner and Benjamin L. Gladd (Peabody, MA: Hendrickson, 2013), 3–30. Block recognizes that he is arguing against a scholarly consensus. The many possible connections between the garden and the later tabernacle/temple, which Block must seek to answer, leave the impression that there is some association between the garden and the temple. One does not have to argue that the garden is a temple, just that there are aspects of the later temple that are an essential part of the garden (in terms of God's presence and the general role of Adam). Block himself recognizes that the garden is a special place, different from the good world God created outside the garden. He also recognizes that the Eden narrative provides much of the conceptual vocabulary for Israel's sanctuary tradition.

to the people (chs. 2–4). In this way they served the priests and kept guard over the tabernacle.

The work of Adam in the garden would not have been exactly the same as the work of the Levites in the tabernacle. The work, or service, of the Levites was on behalf of the priests, to assist them in the details related to the tabernacle. The work of Adam would have included cultivating the garden to grow plants. Yet both are works of service. Significantly, the only two places where these verbs occur together are in reference to Adam's work in the garden and the Levites' work at the tabernacle.[17] The Levites specifically served the priests, and Adam specifically served God. The work of the Levites also served the people, and the work of Adam served his wife and eventually his family and others. Here is the basis of work as a calling or vocation. The guarding of the garden refers to preserving and protecting it. If the garden is a special place of God's presence, guarding it would include protecting the sacred space of the garden just as the Levites protected the sacred space of the tabernacle. The need for this is demonstrated when the serpent approaches Eve with the temptation to disobey God. Adam and Eve should have protected the holiness of the garden by rejecting his offer and putting him out of the garden.

The Role of a Prophet

The prophetic role of Adam and Eve can be shown in how they handle the word of God. Before Eve's creation, God gave Adam a command: "You may surely eat of every tree of the garden, but of the tree of the knowledge of good and evil you shall not eat, for in the day that you eat of it you shall surely die" (Gen. 2:16–17). Clearly, this command was passed on to Eve, because when the serpent approaches her, questioning what God had said about eating from the fruit of the trees, she responds with the command

17. Peter J. Gentry and Stephen J. Wellum, *Kingdom through Covenant* (Wheaton, IL: Crossway, 2012), 211–12.

that God had given to Adam: "You shall not eat of the fruit of the tree that is in the midst of the garden, neither shall you touch it, lest you die" (3:3). Eve's response to the serpent mishandles God's command by adding the phrase "neither shall you touch it." The serpent has raised doubts concerning whether God has their best interests in mind. Eve makes God's command stricter by adding to it. She believes Satan's lie that she can be like God, asserts moral autonomy to choose what is right for herself, eats the fruit, and then gives some to Adam, who also eats. Instead of trusting in God and using his command against Satan's lie, ambiguity concerning what God said results in disobedience. Adam and Eve reject God's word and are disobedient to God's command, which leads to God's judgment.

The Impact of God's Judgment on Prophet, Priest, and King

The judgment of God has a profound effect on creation, on the first couple, and on the mandate that God gave them to fulfill (Gen. 3:8–19). Severe consequences follow when the Word of God is rejected (the prophetic role). Instead of receiving the blessings of God, Adam and Eve experience the judgment of God, which includes being cast out of the garden. They are now separated from him and will be ignorant of his purposes unless he reveals himself. Rejecting the Word of God leaves human beings on their own to establish meaning for their lives (Rom. 2). God will reveal himself to his people, but the pattern of curses following disobedience is built into the Mosaic covenant (Deut. 27–28) and lived out by God's people throughout Israel's history. The clear implication, which is also integral to the Mosaic covenant, is that blessings will accompany obedience to God's Word.

Disobedience also leads to a disruption of fellowship with God, which affects the priestly role. In Genesis 3:8 God came to the garden judging Adam and Eve's sin, but certainly he would have also regularly come to have fellowship with them.[18] Their broken relationship with God is seen when they hide themselves from his presence. Although we are not given any information about the worship of God before the fall, their broken relationship would no doubt affect it. Adam and Eve's feeble attempt to cover themselves with fig leaves is inadequate to cover their guilt and shame.[19] They need God to cover them with animal skins, which implies that blood must be shed for guilt and shame to be covered. Also, instead of the privilege of guarding the garden on God's behalf, Adam and Eve are cast out. The garden is now guarded by the cherubim to keep them from reentering. Work also becomes difficult because the ground is cursed, making it hard to cultivate and produce food. The service aspect of work is disrupted because sin produces selfishness and shifting of blame when Adam and Eve are confronted by God (vv. 11–13). Work also becomes associated with pain and sweat until human beings return to the dust from which they are made. Death is part of the curse.

Adam and Eve also specifically failed in exercising dominion in the garden (the kingly role). They did not protect the garden from opposition, and they did not exercise rule over the serpent by disputing what he said and casting him out. The exercise of dominion becomes difficult because of how sin's curse affects the bearing of children (Gen. 3:16). The mandate to multiply and fill the earth will be attended with sorrow and pain. Enmity between the two seeds, which begins in Genesis 4, includes hostile warfare between the seeds' descendants. Cain murders his brother Abel, and part of his punishment is to be a fugitive and a wanderer, sepa-

18. That God would come regularly into the garden to have fellowship with Adam and Eve is a natural implication from (1) God's creating human beings with the capacity for fellowship, and (2) the form of the verb used in Genesis 3:8 (hitpael of the verb *to walk*), which can imply a regular occurrence. For more discussion on the judgment aspect of Genesis 3:8, see Meredith Kline, *Images of the Spirit* (Eugene, OR: Wipf and Stock, 1980), 102–9.

19. For a discussion of the full effect of sin and how it affects creation and Adam and Eve, see Belcher, *Genesis*, 73–76.

rated from God and other family members who represent the godly line. It is important that worship is mentioned when referring to the godly community (v. 26b). They hope that through this chosen line One will come to battle the enemy and be victorious (3:15).[20]

God's judgment against sin greatly disrupted every aspect of life in the garden, including the mandate and roles that he had given to mankind within creation. The effect of sin on these roles necessitates defining them in a specific and clear way as part of the restoration that God begins after expelling Adam and Eve from the garden. The roles of prophet, priest, and king are formally defined in the establishment of these offices within the nation of Israel. The functions of these roles within Israel are kept separate from each other. There may be minor overlap when the priests teach the people the Word of God or the king takes on a limited role in worship and sacrifice (2 Sam. 6), but for the most part the offices are not mixed. The king is not allowed to go into the tabernacle to offer sacrifices, and when King Uzziah tries to, he is struck with leprosy (2 Chron. 26:16–21). But because the original work given to Adam and Eve included prophetic, priestly, and kingly functions and the roles of prophet, priest, and king are seen in Abraham, they cannot be separated from each other in an absolute sense.[21] This is demonstrated in how the nation of Israel is supposed to fulfill these roles and in how these roles will be united in a coming ruler.

The Mission of Israel and Prophet, Priest, and King

Israel was called by God to fulfill a particular mission to the nations, which can be described with the categories of prophet, priest, and king. Exodus 19:5–6 states that mission just before the establishment of the Mosaic covenant, when Israel will become

---

20. For the argument that Genesis 3:15 includes a single individual, see ibid., 77–78.
21. Herman Bavinck, *Reformed Dogmatics*, vol. 3, *Sin and Salvation in Christ* (Grand Rapids: Baker, 2006), 364–68. He shows that the offices of Christ cannot be completely

a nation based on the law God gives to her. Three terms are used to describe Israel's unique covenant relationship: *treasured possession*, *kingdom of priests*, and *holy nation*. The first term stresses the close relationship that Israel will have to the LORD (Yahweh). *Treasured possession*, which emphasizes that Israel will become Yahweh's unique, prized possession, is also used for a king's personal treasure.[22] The other two terms describe the mediatorial role that Israel will have toward the nations.[23] As a kingdom of priests, Israel will seek to extend the worship and presence of Yahweh. As a holy people, Israel will display what it means to be in a relationship with Yahweh.[24] Israel will fulfill this role by taking the land of Canaan and living for Yahweh in the midst of the nations. God promises to pour out abundant blessing on his people as they trust him and live in obedience to the covenant (Deut. 7:8–16). This will set Israel high above the nations (28:1–14), where she can influence them. They will see the blessing of God upon his people and be drawn to Israel to find out the source. In the process the prophetic aspect will be fulfilled as the nations are taught the benefits of the law of God (4:5–8). The kingly aspect will be fulfilled when Israel becomes a light and extends the rule of God to the nations (Isa. 49:6). All three aspects of prophet, priest, and king are bound together as part of Israel's mission.

That mission did not primarily consist of being sent to the nations; rather, the nations would come to Israel.[25] This was ful-

---

separated from each other, but it is appropriate to make distinctions between them (see also Letham, *The Work of Christ*, 24).

22. John I. Durham, *Exodus* (Waco, TX: Word Books, 1987), 263.

23. Terence E. Fretheim, *Exodus* (Louisville, KY: Westminster John Knox Press, 1991), 212.

24. Durham, *Exodus*, 263.

25. That Israel is not primarily sent to the nations does not deny the OT witness speaking of the Servant's bringing justice to the nations and the psalmist's desire to sing praise among the nations (Pss. 57:9; 108:3). But Israel's main witness was to draw the nations to the God she worshiped. For a discussion of the terms *centripetal* (moving toward the center) and *centrifugal* (moving away from the center) to describe Israel's mission, see Walter C. Kaiser Jr., *Mission in the Old Testament* (Grand Rapids: Baker,

filled to some extent in the early reign of Solomon as the nations, including the queen of Sheba, come to see the great things taking place in Solomon's kingdom (1 Kings 10). But Solomon fell away from the Lord (ch. 11), and the kingdom divided. Israel failed in carrying out this mission, being influenced by the nations rather than influencing the nations (Isa. 2:6-7). Part of Isaiah's teaching states that in light of the failure of God's servant, Israel, to carry out the mission (42:18-19), God must raise up another Servant (49:5). An Anointed One will come to enable Israel to fulfill her mission of being a kingdom of priests (61:5-7), but until this One comes, the mission is kept alive throughout the Old Testament. It is the ideal expressed in Isaiah 2:1-5, and it is the hope of what God can still do after the exile (Zech. 8:20-23). This mission also helps explain how Zechariah 14 and (to some extent) Isaiah 65-66 describe the new heavens and the new earth, where future glories are depicted through Israel's fulfilling this mission. With the coming of Christ, the true Servant of God, the mission of God's people is no longer bound to one geographical area; the disciples are sent to the nations to proclaim the good news of salvation (Matt. 28:19-20; Rom. 4:13).

In the nation of Israel the roles of prophet, priest, and king are basically kept separate to define their meanings. But it is significant that these roles come together in both the description of Adam and Eve and the description of Israel's mission. Thus it makes sense that the Old Testament would begin to describe the coming future ruler as carrying out the combined roles (Ps. 110; Zech. 6:11-13).[26] These are fulfilled in Christ, who is Prophet,

---

2000); Christopher J. H. Wright, *The Mission of God* (Downers Grove, IL: InterVarsity Press, 2006). For a discussion of how Israel was to attract the nations, see Christopher J. H. Wright, *The Mission of God's People* (Grand Rapids: Zondervan, 2010), 128-47.

26. Not everyone agrees that Zechariah 6:11-13 is setting forth the king and the priest as one individual. For the view that they are two separate individuals, see Mark J. Boda, *Haggai, Zechariah* (Grand Rapids: Zondervan, 2004), 336-42. For the view that the king and priest are the same individual, see Eugene H. Merrill, *Haggai, Zechariah, Malachi* (Chicago: Moody Press, 1994), 193-202.

Priest, and King during his earthly ministry. He fulfills them in his work of salvation and continues in these roles on behalf of his people in his ascension. The work of Christ lays the basis for restoring these roles to human beings in their service to God, to the church, and to the world.

Study Questions

1. Do you think it is true that Christians tend to think of Christ's work as one-dimensional? What role do you tend to emphasize?
2. How does Abraham exemplify the roles of prophet, priest, and king?
3. How does the role of a king manifest itself in the place that God gave to human beings at creation? What does it mean that human beings have a kingly role?
4. How does the role of a priest relate to the work that God gave Adam to do in the garden? Since the garden is a special place, what are the implications for the priestly role?
5. How do Adam and Eve exemplify the role of a prophet?
6. How did Adam and Eve fail in the exercise of these roles? What were the implications of this failure?
7. How do the roles of prophet, priest, and king relate to the mission of Israel?

2

The Role of the Prophet
in the Old Testament

PRELIMINARY CONCLUSIONS about the role of a prophet can be drawn from the events before Israel became a nation at Mount Sinai (see chapter 1). The work of the prophet centers on the word of God and prayer. Both of these are evident in Abraham as he receives revelation from God (Gen. 15:1) and prays for Abimelech and his household (ch. 20). Adam and Eve receive revelation from God when he gives them a specific command, but Eve mishandles the word of God when she adds to it. Then the word of God is rejected in favor of the serpent's lie, which is not just a rejection of his word but also a rejection of his authority as Adam and Eve pursue what they think is right for themselves regardless of what God says. This implies that the word of God, which is to be gladly received and obeyed, will lead to great blessings, but the effects of sin make carrying out the prophetic role difficult for human beings. Sin separates humanity from the presence of God and makes it difficult to hear his voice. Although human beings are dependent on God to reveal himself, sin makes it hard to listen to him because of their desire to make their own decisions of right and wrong. But God does not leave humanity in a state of confusion and sets out to restore what was lost at the fall. This restoration includes clearly defining the role of a prophet within the nation of Israel. A clear definition is needed to see how Christ fulfills this role and then how God's people after Christ participate in the prophetic aspect of handling his Word.

The Key Text: Deuteronomy 18:15–22

The roles of prophet, priest, and king have three things in common: texts that define the role, the setting that is in some way a part of the role, and an anointing that is associated with the role. The key text to define the role of the prophet is Deuteronomy 18:15–22. The book of Deuteronomy prepares the people for life in the land of promise. This section lays out covenantal leadership in Canaan.[1] The function of various leaders is presented (judges in 16:18–20, a central tribunal of priests and judges to handle difficult cases in 17:8–13, the king in 17:14–20, and the prophet in 18:15–22).

Divination: Abominable Practices

Just before the role of the prophet is defined, Israel is warned of the abominable practices of the nations who inhabit the land (Deut. 18:9–14). The broad term to describe these methods is *divination* (v. 10, "anyone who practices divination"). This word refers to different ways the nations sought to obtain information from the gods. Sometimes a diviner would use an object to seek information about the future, a method that is called inductive divination. These practices are described in verse 10 as telling

1. Eugene Merrill, *Deuteronomy* (Nashville: Broadman & Holman, 1994), 39. He entitles Deuteronomy 16:18–18:22 "Kingdom Officials" and sees this section as an exposition of the fifth commandment. See also John D. Currid, *A Study Commentary on Deuteronomy* (Darlington, UK: Evangelical Press, 2006).

fortunes, interpreting omens, and being a sorcerer (the NIV [1984] has "engages in witchcraft"). An example of how this might work is given in Ezekiel 21:21–22. The king of Babylon is on the march when he comes to a fork in the road and has to decide whether he should go toward Ammon or toward Jerusalem. To make the decision he uses inductive divination: "He shakes the arrows; he consults the teraphim; he looks at the liver" (v. 21). Each of these practices uses an object to seek the desired information. The shaking of the arrows may refer to reading some sort of configuration of arrows that are thrown to the ground; reading the liver refers to examining the liver of a sacrificial animal; and consulting the teraphim refers to seeking to please a god through an idol in order to then ask that idol questions. This kind of information would be useful to a king, so those able to obtain it would have a position of power.[2] Yet God calls these practices abominations. They are not appropriate for Israel.

Deuteronomy 18:11 also describes the practice of intuitive divination when a diviner becomes a medium to give a message from the gods. These practices refer to consulting the world of the spirits to obtain information. An example is when Saul approached the witch at Endor before a battle with the Philistines, seeking information about the future. It is significant that Saul had already inquired of the LORD (Yahweh), but he had been abandoned by God after rejecting his word. First Samuel 28:6 specifically says that "the LORD did not answer him, either by dreams, or by Urim, or by prophets." These were typical ways that God would communicate with his people. Intuitive divination dealt with the world of the spirits and the dead and is also called an abomination.

Two other abominable practices are mentioned in Deuteronomy 18:9–14. One is child sacrifice. The ESV translates verse 10 as "anyone who burns his son or his daughter as an offering,"

---

2. Bruce K. Waltke, *Finding the Will of God: A Pagan Notion?* (Grand Rapids: Eerdmans, 1995), 29–40.

but it can also be translated as "anyone who makes his son or his daughter pass through the fire." One purpose of child sacrifice was seeking the gods' intervention in life-threatening situations.[3] An example of how the sacrifice of the firstborn son had a dramatic effect on a battle can be seen in 2 Kings 3:27, where the king of Moab offered his oldest son as a burnt offering when the battle was going against him. The other abominable practice is casting spells. The person who casts the spell is called a "charmer" (v. 11). This practice involves trying to gain advantage over someone through prescribed rituals to control the person through a spell. They emphasize manipulating events or people to obtain a favorable outcome. The magicians in Egypt were schooled in such practices.[4]

Because of these abominable practices, God is driving out the nations from the land of Canaan. Israel is not to receive her information from God in these ways. She does not have to manipulate God or situations to seek to control what happens to her; her life is in the hand of a sovereign God who is working out his purposes for the nation. In fact, certain information is off-limits, such as the secret things that belong to the Lord. God will reveal to his people what he wants them to know, and the things revealed "belong to us and to our children forever, that we may do all the words of this law" (Deut. 29:29). This verse speaks of the sufficiency of God's revelation and affirms that he will reveal to his people whatever they need to know. This understanding should give them rest in knowing that he is at work and should help them trust in his sovereign ways. Their focus should be obedience to the word that God reveals. How he will reveal what he wants them to know is presented in Deuteronomy 18:15–22.

3. Currid, *Deuteronomy*, 321. See John Day, *Molech: A God of Human Sacrifice in the Old Testament* (Cambridge: Cambridge University Press, 1989), 82–85.
4. Willem A. VanGemeren, *Interpreting the Prophetic Word* (Grand Rapids: Academie Books, 1990), 19–23. He gives extensive bibliographical references to these practices.

The Definition of a Prophet

Simply, a prophet is someone who speaks the words that God gives him to speak (Deut. 18:18). This definition is basic to the Old Testament view and is confirmed in many places. For example, in Exodus 4:16 Moses makes the excuse that he cannot deliver the people from Egypt because he is not eloquent. God gives him Aaron, whose role is described as speaking to the people the words that Moses gives him. God tells Moses to put the words in Aaron's mouth and Moses will be as God to Aaron. This scenario uses the definition of a prophet to describe Moses' relationship to Aaron and the people (see also Jer. 1:6).

The origin of the prophet's role for Israel goes back to Mount Sinai, where the people saw smoke and fire on the mountain, were afraid that they might die, and sent Moses to talk to God for them. God himself confirmed this arrangement as good (Deut. 18:16–17). Thus a prophet is someone who is a mediator between two sides. On one side is God, and on the other side is the people. God is the superior party in the relationship, and he gives his word—in the form of a message or commands—to the prophet, who then gives that word to the people. This role takes on added significance in the context of the covenant that God establishes with his people. The prophet is God's authorized spokesman.

The main word for *prophet* is *navi* (נביא). It is used in Deuteronomy 18, defining someone who speaks words given to him by God. Two other words used of prophets in the Old Testament put more stress on the subjective aspect of receiving a revelation. The term *roeh* (ראה) comes from the Hebrew verb *to see*, and the term *khozeh* (חזה) comes from the Hebrew verb *to look*. Both terms are translated as *seer*. The emphasis with these terms is that the prophets saw things, either in visions (Amos 1:1) or because they were given access to the divine throne room with the heavenly host standing around the throne (2 Chron. 18:18). Although the latter two terms are not as common as *navi*,[5] all three have the common meaning of "one who speaks the word God gives them," and they can be used interchangeably (1 Chron. 29:29; 2 Chron. 29:25).

False Prophets

The prophet receives the word from God and then speaks that word to the people. This scenario can go wrong in two ways. One way is when the people do not listen to the prophet. But because he speaks the words that God gives to him, it is serious if they do not listen. In Deuteronomy 18:19 God says, "I myself will require it of him." He will hold anyone who does not listen responsible for rejecting his word. The consequences of not listening are further developed in the curses of the covenant (chs. 27–28). Another way in which this scenario can go wrong is when the prophet might not accurately speak the word that God has given to him. Deuteronomy 18 identifies two ways in which this could happen. First, a prophet might presume to speak a word in God's name when God has not commanded him to speak (v. 20). In this situation the prophet claims to speak for God, but it is a false claim because God has not really spoken to the prophet (for examples, see 1 Kings 22 and Jer. 28). Second, a prophet also might speak in the name of a god other than Yahweh (Deut. 18:20). In this case the authority of the prophet is found in a false god (see 1 Kings 18).

There are two responses to false prophets in Deuteronomy 18. First, a false prophet deserves to die. Although this may sound like a harsh punishment, the nation of Israel was to take Canaan and live for God, so that the land was set apart

---

5. The term *navi* is used more than four hundred times in the OT, the term *roeh* is used twelve times, and the term *khozeh* is used sixteen times. Although the terms are interchangeable, *navi* puts more stress on the active work of the prophet in proclaiming the message, and the other two terms put more stress on the subjective aspect of receiving the divine revelation (William White, ראה, *TWOT*, 2:823).

for him. No wickedness or uncleanness was tolerated because it could jeopardize Israel's special relationship with God.[6] A false prophet would lead God's people astray from the Word of God and from the sole worship of God. Such disobedience could not be tolerated because the community of God's people needed to be pure and set apart.

The second response to the false prophet is formulated as a question. It would be easy to identify a false prophet who spoke in the name of another god or who spoke a message that contradicted what God had already revealed to his people. But it would not be as easy to identify a prophet who claimed to speak for God but did not. The people asked how they would know that Yahweh had not spoken through the false prophet. The answer given: if the word that the prophet speaks in the name of Yahweh does not come true, then the prophet has spoken presumptuously. Requiring the prophetic word to come true covers prophecies that can be verified within a period of time. For example, Micaiah prophesied in 1 Kings 22:17 that Ahab would be killed in the upcoming battle with Syria. He even shouted that if Ahab returned in peace, then the Lord had not spoken by him. Whether God spoke by Micaiah would be known shortly. In Jeremiah 28 the prophet Hananiah took yoke bars and spoke in the presence of the people: "Thus says the LORD: Even so I will break the yoke of Nebuchadnezzar king of Babylon from the neck of all nations within two years" (v. 11). This was a false prophecy because the yoke of the king of Babylon was not broken in two years; Jerusalem was destroyed by the Babylonians in about ten years. In summary, there are several ways by which the people could identify a false prophet. A prophet does not speak the word of Yahweh if he speaks in the name of another god, if the word that he speaks contradicts

6. In the new covenant community a false prophet would not be removed by death but by excommunication.

previous revelation, or—assuming that it can be verified—if the word he speaks does not come true.[7]

One Prophet or Many Prophets?

It is clear in the history of Israel that God raised up many prophets for his people. Yet Moses states in Deuteronomy 18:15 that "the LORD your God will raise up for you a prophet like me from among you, from your brothers." The word *prophet* is singular, which raises the question whether this statement includes the prophets who will arise in Israel's history, or only the one Prophet who will arise in the future. It seems clear from Deuteronomy 18 and other texts that this verse cannot be limited to just one prophet.[8] The regulations concerning the identification of a false prophet (vv. 19–22) assume that prophets will arise in the future who will need to be evaluated. Other statements in the Pentateuch compare Moses to the prophets. These statements also use the singular term *prophet* but clearly have in mind other prophets. Numbers 12:6 uses the wording "if there is a prophet among you." This statement cannot be limited to one Prophet who will arise in the future; it refers to any situation when a prophet is raised up by God.

If God's purposes for his people included many prophets, why does Deuteronomy 18:15 use the singular term *prophet* instead of the plural *prophets?* First, the singular term *prophet* can grammatically include a plurality of prophets.[9] Second, the singular

7. For the nature of prophetic proclamation in the context of historical contingencies, which includes how people respond to a prophecy, see Richard Pratt, "Historical Contingencies and Biblical Predictions," in *The Way of Wisdom*, ed. J. I. Packer and Sven K. Sonderlund (Grand Rapids: Zondervan, 2000), 180–203. This article can also be accessed at thirdmill.org.

8. For a robust defense that Deuteronomy 18:15 refers only to the coming Prophet and not to the prophets that arise in Israel's history, see Michael Rydelnik, *The Messianic Hope: Is the Hebrew Bible Really Messianic?* (Nashville: B&H Academic, 2010), 56–64.

9. The singular noun can be a collective form indicating a succession of prophets, which would parallel the use of the word *king* in Deuteronomy 17:14–20. Peter C. Craigie,

term holds open the possibility that in the future one Prophet will arise who will be like Moses. Moses has a special place within the Old Testament. God speaks to him face-to-face (Num. 12:8; Deut. 34:10), and the signs and wonders he did in the land of Egypt stand far above any work of any other prophet in the Old Testament (Deut. 34:10–12). Deuteronomy 18:15 and the statement that there has not risen a prophet in Israel like Moses give hope that one day a Prophet will arise like Moses. God will speak face-to-face with this Prophet and will use him to accomplish great signs and wonders.

Moses and the Prophets

Moses' special place within the Old Testament economy can also be seen in the foundational role that the Mosaic covenant plays in relationship to the prophets of Israel's history. The history of Israel is laid out in several places in Deuteronomy: the disobedience of God's people will lead to exile, but then God will bring his people back to the land to restore them (see Deut. 29–30, 32). This general history is also set forth in the curses of the Mosaic covenant (27:11–26; 28:15–68), which describe what will happen in the future if God's people disobey, including being exiled from their land. The covenant also laid out all the wondrous ways that God would bless his people for their faithfulness (28:1–14). When Israel breaks the covenant, God sends the prophets as covenant mediators to call his people back to him and warn them of the judgment that they would experience if they continued to disobey. The prophets became covenant prosecutors sent by God to bring a complaint against the people for their disobedience and to hold out blessings if they repented.[10]

The Book of Deuteronomy (Grand Rapids: Eerdmans, 1976), 262n18.

10. For general issues related to the covenant lawsuit, see Herbert B. Huffmon, "The Covenant Lawsuit in the Prophets," *JBL* 78 (1959): 286–95. For discussion of the definition of the word *riv* (ריב) and its use in international relationships and in the

Although the prophets received direct revelation from God, they also preached the stipulations of the Mosaic covenant to the people.[11] Jeremiah is specifically told to proclaim the words of the covenant in the cities of Judah and in the streets of Jerusalem (Jer. 11:6). Covenant blessings can be broken down into two broad categories. Blessings in nature include agricultural plenty, livestock fertility, health, prosperity, and population increase. Blessings in warfare include the defeat of enemies, the end of warfare, relief from destruction, and return from exile.[12] Covenant judgment can also be broken down into two categories. Judgment in nature includes drought, pestilence, famine, disease, wild animals, and population loss. Judgment in warfare includes defeat, siege, occupation, death, destruction, and exile.[13] Specific stipulations of the curses are used by the prophet to warn the people of coming judgment. Deuteronomy 28:30 states, "You shall build a house, but you shall not dwell in it," and Zephaniah 1:13 reflects this: "Though they build houses, they shall not inhabit them."[14] In this way the prophets preached the Mosaic covenant to the people of God.

The Important Role of the Prophet in Israel

The prophets are not the only way that God communicated with his people. First Samuel 28:6 mentions the legitimate ways

Prophets, see James Limburg, "The Root רִיב and the Prophetic Lawsuit Speeches," *JBL* 88 (1969): 291–304.

11. For a discussion of the relationship of Deuteronomy to the structure of the Hittite international treaties of the second millennium, see Meredith Kline, *Treaty of the Great King* (Grand Rapids: Eerdmans, 1963); K. A. Kitchen, *On the Reliability of the Old Testament* (Grand Rapids: Eerdmans, 2003).

12. These categories come from Richard Pratt, *He Gave Us Prophets* videos, Third Millennium Ministries, 1999. See also Douglas Stuart, who lists ten covenant blessings. *Hosea–Jonah* (Dallas: Word Books, 1987), xli–lii.

13. Pratt, *He Gave Us Prophets*. See also Stuart, who lists twenty-seven types of covenant judgment (*Hosea–Jonah*, xxxi–xl).

14. For more examples from Zephaniah 1, see O. Palmer Robertson, *The Books of Nahum, Habakkuk, and Zephaniah* (Grand Rapids: Eerdmans, 1990), 254–55. If Zephaniah

THE ROLE OF THE PROPHET IN THE OLD TESTAMENT

that God might have spoken to King Saul, including dreams, Urim, and prophets. God used dreams to communicate with both Israelites (Jacob in Gen. 28:10–17; Solomon in 1 Kings 3:5, 15; and Joseph in Matt. 1:20) and non-Israelites (Abimelech in Gen. 20; two Midianite soldiers in Judg. 7; and the Magi in Matt. 2). Numbers 12:6 identifies dreams, along with visions, as the ways in which God would speak to a prophet. Sometimes dreams had to be interpreted, with the source of the interpretation coming from God (Gen. 41; Dan. 2). Downsides to dreams included that they can be fleeting (Job 20:8), they might be caused by the cares of this world (Eccl. 5:3), and they can be deceptively used by false prophets who claim to have revelation from God (Jer. 29:8–9).

God also used the Urim and Thummim (UT) to communicate with his people. Although there is a lot about the UT that we do not know, they were associated with the ephod of the priests and were used to make decisions concerning the nation.[15] They were used by Joshua to know when to go out to battle (Num. 27:21), and David used them to inquire of the Lord concerning various decisions early in his reign. For example, he used them to find out whether the city of Keilah would deliver him into the hands of Saul (1 Sam. 23:6) and whether he should pursue the Amalekites, who had raided the city of Ziklag and carried off the families of David and his men. The UT are also mentioned in Ezra 2 as a way to determine the ancestry of the priests who returned from exile (v. 63).

---

is specifically quoting from the curses of the book of the covenant, this would support a date for Zephaniah after the discovery of the book of the law in 621 B.C. Another example of a prophet's preaching the curses of the covenant to the people is Ezekiel 5:10–17, which uses terminology from Leviticus 26:22–33.

15. The UT appear to be two stone pieces connected to the breastplate of the high priest (called the breastpiece of judgment) that was attached to the ephod. How the two stones were used to make decisions is not known. For a review of how they are understood to function, see Cornelius Van Dam, *The Urim and Thummim: A Means of Revelation in Ancient Israel* (Winona Lake, IN: Eisenbrauns, 1997), 9–38. The UT were a divinely ordained method of inductive divination used when the leader or king needed to make a decision that related to the nation. The UT were probably in view if a king was said to inquire of the Lord.

Although dreams, UT, and prophets were the legitimate ways that God would communicate with his people, the role of the prophet emerged as the main way that God revealed his purposes. Although he communicated with individuals, primarily kings, through dreams, dreams were also a way in which God would speak to a prophet (Num. 12:6). In this way dreams and prophets were bound together. The UT are mentioned in connection with Joshua and David, but their use disappears with the rise of prophets in Israel. Prophets became the primary way that God revealed himself to his people.[16] Amos affirms this when he writes, "For the Lord GOD does nothing without revealing his secret to his servants the prophets" (3:7).

Called by God

The Old Testament prophet's major role as the primary way that God would speak to his people is supported by several other factors. The prophets were set apart through a call from God. Some prophets specifically mention their call, including Isaiah, Jeremiah, and Ezekiel. Several components are common to the call. First, it is clear when the prophet is called. Jeremiah is told by God that he was appointed as a prophet before he was born (Jer. 1:5). All three prophets are told that they were being sent to a rebellious people who would not necessarily receive their message from God. The prophets were not, however, to be afraid of the people's rejection, words, or even looks in reaction to the prophets' message (vv. 16–19; Ezek. 2:4–7). Second, the prophets emphasized their inadequacy to

---

16. For the evidence of professional prophets who speak in the name of a deity and how they functioned in the ANE, see J. Stokl, "Ancient Near Eastern Prophecy," in *Dictionary of the Old Testament Prophets*, ed. Mark J. Boda and J. Gordon McConville (Downers Grove, IL: InterVarsity Press, 2013), 16–24. The function of the prophets in Israel had several unique features: they emerged as the main way in which God spoke to his people, their function extended over a long period of time, they had a more antagonistic relationship to the king, and they left a written legacy unmatched in the ANE. See also Abraham Malamat, "Prophecy at Mari," in *The Place Is Too Small for Us*, ed. Robert P. Gordon (Winona Lake, IN: Eisenbrauns, 1995), 50–73.

fulfill their prophetic role, often accompanied by excuses. When Isaiah saw the glory of God's holiness, he exclaimed, "Woe is me" (Isa. 6:5). Jeremiah protested that he did not know how to speak because he was only a youth (Jer. 1:6). In Ezekiel there is tension as to whether he will accept the call (Ezek. 3:14–15).[17] He is told not to be rebellious like the people of God, he is made to eat the scroll (v. 1), and he is told the seriousness of the responsibility of a prophet to be a watchman (vv. 16–21). Finally, once a prophet is called, he feels constrained by the call to speak the word of God. This is seen most clearly in Jeremiah, who faced a difficult situation because of the way he was treated by the people who rejected his message (Jer. 11:21; 20:1–6). Even in hardship God's words were a joy and delight (15:16), and he was unable to refrain from speaking them (20:9). The call of the prophet emphasized his important role within God's redemptive program.

Anointed with Oil

Evidence shows that at least some of the prophets were anointed with oil. Although the evidence is not as extensive as it is with the priests and kings, there is one clear instance in which a prophet is anointed for service. Elijah is told to anoint Elisha so that he would be a prophet to take Elijah's place (1 Kings 19:16). The other passage[18] in the Old Testament that might indicate prophets' being anointed is Psalm 105:15, which states, "Touch not my anointed ones, do my prophets no harm!" The parallelism in this verse seems to identify the anointed ones with the prophets.

---

17. For the view that Ezekiel is resisting the call in Ezekiel 3:14–15, see Daniel I. Block, *The Book of Ezekiel: Chapters 1–24* (Grand Rapids: Eerdmans, 1997), 135–38.

18. There are too many questions surrounding Zechariah 4:14 to use it as a text that confirms the anointing of the prophets. Even if the two olive trees that supply oil for the lampstand are prophets (see Mark Boda, *Haggai, Zechariah* [Grand Rapids: Zondervan, 2004], 274–75), "sons of oil" (literal translation) in verse 14 may not signify anointing (a different term for *oil* is used for the anointing oil). It may refer to oil supplied by the prophets for the lampstand.

Psalm 105 is a review of the history of Israel, and verse 15 occurs in the review of the patriarchal period, making this a reference to the patriarchs. The plural forms indicate that not just Abraham is in view. He is called a prophet in Genesis 20:7, and this designation can also be applied to Isaac and Jacob. No evidence shows that the patriarchs were anointed with oil, so this may be a metaphorical use of anointing, showing that Yahweh had claimed them as his own and that they were under his protection.[19] Calvin argues that these terms in verse 15 refer to the people of God, who were few in number and wandered from nation to nation (vv. 12–13).[20] If this passage is referring more broadly to the people of God and not just to the patriarchs, it foreshadows (1) the prophetic role that the nation of Israel will fulfill and (2) the later use of *anointed* to refer to the people of God after the coming of Christ. Clearly, anointing with oil is closely associated with being a prophet, even if that anointing does not happen to every prophet. The anointing emphasizes that prophets are set apart for God. One can see here, at least in a general sense, the internal call confirmed by some kind of external recognition.

The Emergence of the Prophets in the History of Israel

Early in Israel's history, in the book of Judges, the prophets were raised up by God to warn Israel of the consequences of disobedience. During the days of Joshua, the Lord gave instructions directly (Josh. 3:7; 4:15; 5:2; 6:2; 8:1, 18; 13:1); both the identification of Achan as the one who took the devoted things from the spoils of Jericho and the distribution of the land among the tribes were done by lot.[21] At the beginning of the book of Judges the people inquire of the Lord which tribe should go up first to

19. John Goldingay, *Psalms 1–41* (Grand Rapids: Baker, 2006), 209.
20. John Calvin, *Psalms 93–150* (Grand Rapids: Baker, 1996), 182–83.
21. For a good discussion of the difference between the lot and the UT, see Van Dam, *Urim and Thummim*, 215–18.

fight against the Canaanites. Their method of inquiring of the Lord is not specified, but it could have been the UT. When Israel failed to drive out the Canaanites, the angel of Yahweh was sent to warn the people of the consequences of their disobedience (Judg. 2:1–5). Then in Judges 6:7–10 the Lord sent a prophet to warn the people when they cried out to him. The prophet's message is similar to the earlier message of the angel of Yahweh: God has delivered his people from Egypt and has given them the land, but they have not obeyed him. The role of the prophet to speak God's warning to his people goes back to Moses and becomes prominent in the work of future prophets.

Samuel is a transitional figure standing between the period of the judges and the period of the monarchy. He functions as a priest, a judge, and a prophet. He was raised up by God at a time when the people needed leadership at the national level (Judg. 17:6) and at the priestly level, because the sons of Eli were wicked (1 Sam. 2:12–17). The Lord even sent a prophet, called "a man of God," to rebuke Eli for his sons' wickedness and to proclaim the coming disaster upon them. Even though a prophet is sent to Eli with this message of condemnation, 1 Samuel 3:1 says that the word of Yahweh was rare in those days. As a boy, Samuel was ministering to Yahweh in the presence of Eli, and when the Lord called to Samuel, he did not recognize it as the Lord but thought Eli was calling him. Eli concluded that it was the Lord speaking with Samuel, and so Samuel responded with: "Speak, for your servant hears" (v. 10). God then declared to Samuel how he was going to punish the house of Eli. This began the prophetic ministry of Samuel, who had the presence of the Lord, and the Lord gave success to his words (v. 19).[22] Thus everyone from Dan to Beersheba knew that Samuel was established as a prophet. Samuel's prophetic ministry was demonstrated early when he

---

22. Both the words of the "man of God" and the word that God gave to Samuel about the house of Eli came to pass (1 Sam. 4:10–22).

received the word of God (7:9), spoke the word of God to the people (vv. 3–4), and prayed for the people (v. 5).

The Prophet and the King

The establishment of a king in Israel elevated the role of the prophet. The relationship between the prophet and the king is highlighted in Samuel's farewell address to Israel (1 Sam. 12). Samuel asserts his integrity before the people; warns them, based on their history, of the dangers of disobedience; and exhorts them to fear the Lord, obey his voice, and not rebel against his commandment. If they do these things, it will be well with them, but if they do not, the Lord will be against them and their king. Both the people and the king are to obey the Lord. The importance of this is played out in the kingship of Saul. When Saul disobeyed the word of the Lord by Samuel in 1 Samuel 13, he lost the prospect of an eternal kingdom (v. 13). When he disobeyed the Lord a second time by not destroying the Amalekites and their king (ch. 15), God rejected him as king. The king must submit himself to the word of God, or the king will be judged by God. This means that the king must submit to the prophet who speaks the word of God.

Not many prophets are mentioned during the kingship of David, perhaps because David was, for the most part, a godly king. David used the UT for decisions related to warfare (1 Sam. 23:1–2) and the kingship (2 Sam. 2:1–2). The prophet Nathan assumed a role related to the Davidic covenant and to David's sin with Bathsheba. Regarding the Davidic covenant, he revealed from God why David will not build the temple. He also told David that God wanted to build him a house/dynasty, with the promise of a descendant who would sit on the throne forever. Regarding David's sin, Nathan confronted him, pronounced God's forgiveness, told him that the child will die, and affirmed God's love for Solomon—another son whom Bathsheba bore to David. The prophet Gad is also mentioned in connection to David. He helped when David was fleeing Saul (1 Sam. 22:5), he presented the word of the Lord to David concerning the punishments he could choose from after the census (2 Sam. 24:11–14), and he encouraged David to build an altar to the Lord on the thresh-ing floor of Araunah to halt the punishment (vv. 18–19). There is little evidence that Nathan or Gad spoke to the people. Their ministry was mainly to the king; in fact, Gad is called David's seer (v. 11). These prophets function like court advisers, but it is clear that they speak the word of God to the king.

Not many prophets were involved in the reign of Solomon. Nathan was involved in the establishment of his kingship, but many times the Lord spoke directly to him. Later in his reign, after Solomon turned away from the Lord, God raised up the prophet Ahijah to tell Jeroboam that he would reign over ten tribes of Israel. Once the kingdom was divided, the prophets became outsiders to the royal court because many times they brought a message of God's judgment to the king and people. Many faithful prophets were raised up by God to serve in the early days of the divided kingdom. Several of them were anony-mous (1 Kings 20:13; 2 Kings 9:1–4).[23] Jeroboam I, the first king of the northern kingdom, set that kingdom's path on the road to apostasy when he set up his own centers of worship in Dan and Bethel (1 Kings 12:25–33). The height of apostasy was reached in the days of Ahab and Jezebel with their commitment to Baal worship. This false commitment to Baal spilled over into the southern kingdom (2 Kings 8:16–19; 11:1–3), and many kings in the southern kingdom were also disobedient to God and encouraged false worship (Ahaz, Manasseh, Jehoahaz, Jehoiakim, Zedekiah). God responded to this covenant disobedience by raising up the prophets, who spoke his message in difficult situations.

23. For a list of the prophets who served during the days of the divided kingdom, see VanGemeren, *Interpreting the Prophetic Word*, 49.

The School of the Prophets

The prophets' significant role becomes clear in the emergence of the school of the prophets, the ministries of Elijah and Elisha, and the legacy of the writing prophets. Little is known about the school of the prophets. The first mention of a group of prophets is in the anointing of Saul as king (1 Sam. 10:10–13). A group of prophets met Saul, and the Spirit of God rushed on him and he prophesied with them. No information is given for the origin of this group, but in a similar incident later in Saul's life (19:20–24), a company of prophets led by Samuel is mentioned. It is likely that Samuel had something to do with organizing this company. The word of the Lord was rare at the beginning of Samuel's life (3:1), and these prophets may have been raised up by God and organized by Samuel to meet the situations that would develop in the early days of the kingship of Saul and later in the divided kingdom. They were certainly prominent during the crises faced by Elijah and Elisha.

The function of the school of the prophets can only be surmised from the little that is said in the Scriptures.[24] The first activity mentioned is "prophesying" (1 Sam. 10:10–13). It is unclear exactly what this activity involves,[25] but the Spirit of God rushed on Saul and he prophesied among the prophets. One implication of this incident at the beginning of the kingship of Saul is that the newly appointed king was to be subordinate to the Spirit and

24. For a perceptive discussion of the sons of the prophets, see the older work by Hobart E. Freeman, *An Introduction to the Old Testament Prophets* (Chicago: Moody Press, 1968), 28–34; see also P. A. Verhoef, "Prophecy," in *NIDOTTE*, 4:1073.

25. Many argue that the prophets of Israel engaged in ecstatic activity based on ANE parallels (Moshe Weinfeld, "Ancient Near Eastern Patterns in Prophetic Literature," in *The Place Is Too Small for Us*, 35–37). For the view that the prophets were not engaging in ecstatic behavior and that the use of musical instruments was a way to praise God, see Leon J. Wood, *The Holy Spirit in the Old Testament* (Eugene, OR: Wipf and Stock, 1998), 101–12. Wood acknowledges that a strong emotional involvement is related to this activity. Others are more willing to allow for some kind of divinely induced revelatory experience that would be different from that of the pagan prophets. Ronald F. Youngblood, "1–2 Samuel," in *The Expositor's Bible Commentary*, ed. Frank E. Gaebelein (Grand Rapids: Zondervan, 1992), 3:624–25; Edward J. Young, *My Servants the Prophets* (Grand Rapids: Eerdmans, 1952), 86.

the prophetic word.[26] The connection of *prophesy* with the use of musical instruments (1 Chron. 25:1–5) implies that prophesying includes praising God. Praising God has a prophetic aspect because praise includes God's exaltation, but prophesying also includes warning and admonition. During the famine and the emergence of Baal worship under Ahab, the prophets found comfort, help, and fellowship in living together (2 Kings 6:1–7).[27] Possibly training took place; at least they would learn together as they watched the ministries of Elijah and Elisha. Elisha uses one of the sons of the prophets to anoint Jehu as king of Israel (9:1–5).

The Ministries of Elijah and Elisha

The back-to-back ministries of Elijah and Elisha are significant for the history of Israel, but they also have implications for redemptive history. Elijah specifically confronted the worship of Baal that was supported by King Ahab and Jezebel. The three-year famine was a direct attack on Baal, who was the storm god. The confrontation of Elijah with the prophets of Baal on Mount Carmel showed that Yahweh was God, not Baal. The ministry of Elijah demonstrated what a true prophet should be as he stood faithfully for Yahweh and against the worship of false gods. He called the king and God's people to faithful obedience to the

26. A similar incident occurs later in Saul's reign as he is pursuing David. By this time Saul had rejected the word of God and thus had been rejected by God as king. In 1 Samuel 19 Saul sent messengers after David; they were overcome by the Spirit of God and prophesied with the prophets. Finally, Saul himself came and he too prophesied after the Spirit of God came on him. Unlike the first time that Saul prophesied (ch. 10), this was not a positive experience. Saul stripped off his clothes and lay naked all day and night. Such an experience was not mentioned concerning the other messengers whom Saul had sent. This shows Saul resisting God's will concerning the rejection of his kingship and the elevation of David. In despair and melancholy, Saul realized that there was little hope for his kingship, but he continued to fight the will of God. Wood, *Holy Spirit in the Old Testament*, 106.

27. Freeman, *Introduction to the Old Testament Prophets*, 30–34. He notes that the sons of the prophets were supported by the gifts of the people, lived in common dwellings, and primarily performed a religious service.

covenant. Just as Moses became identified with the Torah, Elijah embodied the prophets as one who would appear before the great and terrible day of the Lord (Mal. 4:4–6).

Elisha was Elijah's successor, and he received a double portion of Elijah's spirit. His ministry was noted for its many miracles, which established him as an authentic prophet and the true successor to Elijah (2 Kings 2:13–15). His miracles included helping the band of the prophets (6:1–7), thwarting the plans of the enemy in divine warfare (vv. 8–23), multiplying bread for the sons of the prophets (4:42–44), and raising the dead (vv. 8–37). Elisha's ministry paralleled Elijah's, but there were differences. Elijah was mainly used by God to confront his people in their worship of Baal. Elisha's ministry emphasized encouraging the faithful remnant and reminding people that God is the One who delivers. Both show that God has power over death (1 Kings 17:17–24; 2 Kings 4:18–37). The ministries of Elijah and Elisha set up an interesting parallel between John the Baptist and Jesus (see chapter 3).

The Writing Prophets

It is hard to overestimate the importance of the writing prophets' legacy in their passion for God, their boldness in proclamation, and their literary compositions' complexity. Nothing compares to them in the ancient Near East. The purpose here is to highlight their work related to the role of the prophet. In Amos the close relationship between Yahweh and the prophet is brought out in the pronouncement of covenant curses. Amos presents Yahweh like a lion who roars from Zion (Amos 1:2) as he comes to pronounce judgment. Instead of God's sending wild beasts against his people (Lev. 26:22), Yahweh himself shows up as the "wild beast." The role of the prophet is to proclaim the roar of the lion. When the lion roars, there is fear; when God has spoken, the prophets must prophesy (Amos 3:8) because God reveals his secrets to them (v. 7). In Isaiah 6 the impact of the prophetic message is given after Isaiah sees the holiness of God and is commissioned as a prophet. He is told that the prophetic word will lead to a judicial hardening of God's people (vv. 9–10). In this way the word of God accomplishes the purposes for which God has ordained it (55:10–11). Those purposes include both salvation (vv. 12–13) and judgment (6:9–10). In Ezekiel the responsibility of the prophet is emphasized when the prophet is identified as a watchman (3:16–21; 33:1–9). The important role of the watchman was to warn a city of a coming enemy. The watchman had the responsibility to warn the people of God so that they might turn from their wickedness. If a prophet failed to warn God's people of their sin, then not only would the people die but the prophet would be held responsible for their blood. To fulfill such a ministry, the prophets were dependent on the Holy Spirit, who had given them the power to proclaim to "Jacob his transgression and to Israel his sin" (Mic. 3:8).

Opposition to the Prophets

The calling of prophets was difficult because of the opposition they faced. They had to be committed to God above everything else, because the prophets put their lives on the line for the sake of the truth of God's word. They identified with the cause of God so closely because his word became part of their lives. Ezekiel was told to eat the scroll (3:1), and Jeremiah declared that the word of God was shut up in his bones (20:9). Both Ezekiel and Jeremiah were told not to be afraid when they faced opposition, not even to be afraid of their faces (Jer. 1:8; Ezek. 2:4),[28] as they proclaimed the truth of God's word. Prophets had to develop a tough skin, because many would fight against them and their message (Jer. 1:16–19). Ezekiel lost his wife, the desire of his eyes (Ezek. 24:15–24), which became a lesson to the people of God that they too would lose what they loved when Jerusalem was destroyed.

28. Jeremiah 1:8 literally reads "their faces."

Jeremiah also suffered greatly as a prophet. Although he had the support of some people at various times in his ministry (Jer. 26:16–19), it seemed that everyone was against him. Not only was he opposed by priests, false prophets, and the kings of Judah (20:1–4; 28:5–16; 32:1–5), but even Jeremiah's family and the men of his hometown of Anathoth were against him (11:21–23). He described himself as "a gentle lamb led to the slaughter" (v. 19). He was considered a traitor, because as the fall of Jerusalem drew near he proclaimed that the people should surrender to the Babylonians (21:1–10). The sufferings of Jeremiah led to several laments in which he expressed the depths of his pain. He had been ostracized by everyone so that he sat alone, separated from the rest of society (15:17). He even wished that he had not been born (20:14–18). Jeremiah struggled with the word God gave to him. On the one hand, the word had become a reproach to him—so much so that he decided not to speak anymore in God's name. But he could not refrain because the word of God was a burning fire within him that could not be contained (v. 9). On the other hand, it was the joy and delight of his heart (15:16). Jeremiah also struggled with his relationship with God; at times he felt abandoned. He even expressed that he could not count on God, who was like a deceitful brook with no water (v. 18). Jeremiah did not fully comprehend what being a prophet would entail because God called him when he was young (20:7). Of course, he also knew the goodness and grace of God. Although God spared his life, other prophets were put to death (26:20–23). The prophets suffered greatly for the sake of the truth of God's word.

The Prophet and Prayer

The prophet was also to intercede for others. Abraham was called a prophet (Gen. 20:7) specifically regarding his role of intercession. He interceded for Sodom and Gomorrah that God's judgment would not destroy the righteous with the wicked (18:22–33).

He prayed for the household of Abimelech that God would take away the barrenness that God had sent to protect Sarah (20:11–17). Pharaoh asked Moses to pray to Yahweh because he recognized Moses' mediatorial role in relationship to the plagues (Ex. 8:8–15; 9:27–35; 10:17–20). Moses interceded for Miriam when she was struck with leprosy for opposing him (Num. 12:13–15). Even though Samuel did not agree with the people's request for a king, he committed himself to pray for them; in fact, he notes that it would be a sin against the Lord if he did not pray for them.

The prophet was to have a ministry of prayer. He should pray for God's people, even when they have rejected the word of God or acted in disobedience. Intercession was often a role of pleading with God to show mercy to people instead of showing them the judgment they deserve. Thus it is rather shocking to hear God tell Jeremiah several times not to pray for the people (Jer. 7:16; 11:14; 14:11–12). This assumes that Jeremiah would be carrying out the regular role of intercession. It also gives insight into the times in which Jeremiah lived. During the closing days of the southern kingdom it became inevitable that judgment was going to fall on Judah, and at that point, prayer was no longer necessary because there was no possibility that God's judgment could be averted. Clearly, the ministry of the prophets consisted of the word of God and prayer.

The Coming of a Future Prophet

A view developed in the Old Testament that God would send his people a Prophet who will usher in a coming day of restoration. Deuteronomy 18:15 states that God will send a Prophet like Moses to the people, and Deuteronomy 34:10–12 asserts that such a Prophet has not yet arisen in Israel. The figure in Isaiah 61 can be associated with the role of the prophet because he proclaims the good news of God's salvation. Joel speaks of a coming day when the Spirit of God will be poured out upon God's people so that sons and daughters, young and old, and male and female servants will prophesy. This wider ability to prophesy goes back to an incident in Numbers 11 when Moses complains about the burden of meeting the people's expectations. God helps by setting apart seventy elders and by sending the Spirit upon them so that they prophesied. When someone complained that two men remained in the camp prophesying, Moses responded, "Would that all the Lord's people were prophets, that the Lord would put his Spirit on them!" This is the hope expressed in Joel 2, which awaits the coming of the awesome day of the Lord when everyone who calls on the name of the Lord will be saved (vv. 31–32). Malachi 4:5 speaks of this same day, which will be preceded by the coming of Elijah the prophet who will begin the process of reconciliation "before the great and awesome day of the LORD."

Study Questions

1. Define *divination* and list some of its practices. Why does God call such practices abominations?
2. How would you define *prophet*? What do the different words used for *prophet* emphasize?
3. How can a false prophet be identified? How did God's people respond to false prophets?
4. Discuss the implications of the singular use of *prophet* in Deuteronomy 18:15.
5. How do the prophets preach the Mosaic covenant to the nation of Israel?
6. Discuss the role of the UT.
7. How were the prophets set apart for their ministry?
8. Discuss the role of the prophet in relationship to the king.
9. Why were the ministries of Elijah and Elisha important?
10. How do the opposition to the prophets and the importance of prayer relate to pastoral ministry?

3

CHRIST AS PROPHET:
MIGHTY IN WORD AND DEED

WHEN JOHN THE BAPTIST came preaching that people must repent, "for the kingdom of heaven is at hand," many wondered who he was. The priests and Levites from Jerusalem even asked him, "Who are you?" (John 1:19). In their conversation they also asked him, "Are you the Prophet?" (v. 21). It is clear that people were looking for the coming Prophet. This hope goes back to the promise of Deuteronomy 18:15 and the desire for this Prophet in Deuteronomy 34:10–12. Clear statements later in Israel's history show that prophetic revelation had ceased. During the Maccabean period, the cessation of prophecy is acknowledged (1 Macc. 4:46; 9:27; 14:41); in fact, the period of prophetic activity had long ceased by that time.[1] People in the first century were looking for

1. Roger Beckwith, *The Old Testament Canon of the New Testament Church and Its Background in Early Judaism* (Grand Rapids: Eerdmans, 1985), 372. He shows that awareness of prophecy's cessation was acknowledged by almost all the Jewish schools of thought (383–85, 399). For a brief discussion of the rise of Jewish apocalyptic literature and its relationship to written prophecy, see Ronald E. Clements, *Old Testament Prophecy* (Louisville, KY: Westminster John Knox Press, 1996), 177–88.

the Prophet who would end God's silence, speak God's word, and restore God's people.

The Ministry of John the Baptist

John the Baptist was not the Prophet, but he had a significant role to play in preparing the way for and witnessing to the Prophet. John understood his role as preparing the way of the Lord (Isa. 40:3; Matt. 3:1–3). He accomplished this in the Judean wilderness by proclaiming the coming of the kingdom and by baptizing those who confessed their sin. John even reluctantly baptized Jesus, not because Jesus had sin to confess but "to fulfill all righteousness" (Matt. 3:15). Jesus had to be baptized to fulfill the law and to identify with sinners.[2] His baptism also launched his public ministry, with a declaration from heaven confirming that he was the Son of God. This can be considered Jesus' call to ministry in line with the prophets of old.[3] Confirmation of this call comes in a number of ways, but at the Mount of Transfiguration the prophetic role of Jesus is confirmed. Two Old Testament figures, Moses and Elijah, appear with Jesus on the mount. They represent the Law and the Prophets that give witness to him, but both figures are also prophets. Moses is the foundational prophet of the old covenant. He is the type of prophet that the people hoped God would send to them (Deut. 18:15). Elijah stood firm for the truth of God in the face of apostasy. When Peter suggests that he build three tents, one for each of them, a voice from the cloud exclaims, "This is my beloved Son, with whom I am well pleased; listen to him" (Matt. 17:5). Someone greater than Moses and Elijah is here. Someone greater than the great prophets of old is here. The directive "listen to him" means that he is the One through whom God would speak. He is the One

2. Herman N. Ridderbos, *Matthew* (Grand Rapids: Zondervan, 1987), 58–59.
3. The call of Christ also included his anointing, not by literal oil but by the Holy Spirit, who descended like a dove and rested on him at his baptism.

who will reveal the purposes and revelation of God. He is the Prophet to whom God's people must listen.

The ministry of John the Baptist prepares the way for the coming of the Lord. Although John denies that he is Elijah (John 1:21), Jesus affirms that John is fulfilling the role of Elijah in his ministry of preparation for the coming One.[4] This ministry is in accordance with Malachi 4:5–6, which states that God would send Elijah the prophet before the great and terrible day of the Lord. His ministry will be a ministry of reconciliation to turn the hearts of fathers to their children and the hearts of children to their fathers. This is not just a restoration of the social order but the restoration of the covenant itself.[5] John preaches a message of repentance and confession so that people can be right with God in preparation for the coming One. He is much like Elijah in his ministry of confrontation, especially toward the leaders of the Jewish people (Matt. 3:7–10).

John also speaks of the ministry of the coming One in prophetic terms. While John baptizes only with water for repentance, the One who comes will baptize with the Holy Spirit and fire. The outpouring of the Holy Spirit is associated with the prophets and prophetic activity in the Old Testament (Num. 11:26–30; Joel 2:28–29). The One who comes will baptize with the Holy Spirit, and there will be an increase of prophetic activity among God's people. John also proclaims that the One who comes will come in judgment. He will clear the threshing floor with his winnowing hook, will baptize with fire—a figure of judgment—and will burn the chaff (Matt. 3:11–12). He will also come to gather the wheat into the barn, a picture of the salvation of his people. John, like the prophets of old, saw the two aspects of the day of the Lord as happening in one great event that would bring an end to history.

4. For a discussion of John's denial and Jesus' affirmation that John is Elijah, see Leon Morris, *The Gospel according to John* (Grand Rapids: Eerdmans, 1971), 134–35.

5. Pieter A. Verhof, *The Books of Haggai and Malachi* (Grand Rapids: Eerdmans, 1987), 342.

CHRIST AS PROPHET: MIGHTY IN WORD AND DEED

As John languishes in prison and hears of the deeds of Christ, he sends his disciples to Jesus to ask whether he is really the One or whether they should look for another. Perhaps John did not see judgment in the ministry of Jesus. But Jesus' response emphasizes the deeds of salvation that are being accomplished. He ends with the words, "And blessed is the one who is not offended by me" (11:6). The offense may have to do with the grace of salvation that comes to sinners through Jesus. The great day of judgment will be delayed so that his kingdom can spread over all the earth.[6] The ministry of John the Baptist is a prophetic ministry like that of Elijah the prophet, and his testimony is that the One who comes will also carry out the ministry of a prophet.

A Prophet like Moses

Jesus is identified by the two men on the road to Emmaus as a Prophet mighty in word and deed (Luke 24:19). Many parallels between Moses and Jesus confirm that he is the Prophet "like me" (Deut. 18:15) sent from God. Unlike the other prophets, Moses experienced God speaking to him clearly and directly, even face-to-face (34:10). Jesus had an even closer relationship to the God of Moses, his own Father. Before the world began he was in his presence and shared his glory (John 17:5). Moses performed mighty deeds in the deliverance of Israel from Egypt, and Jesus performed miracles in the deliverance of his people from the power of sin and death. Moses' face shone after speaking with God on Mount Sinai, and in Jesus' transfiguration his clothes became white and "his face shone like the sun" (Matt. 17:2). These parallels show that Jesus is the Prophet "like Moses," but (1) he

6. This delay of judgment is confirmed when Jesus reads from the prophet Isaiah in the synagogue and he stops reading after the phrase "to proclaim the year of the Lord's favor" (Luke 4:19, quoting Isa. 61:2). The very next phrase, which Jesus does not read, is "and the day of vengeance of our God" (Isa. 61:2). Jesus comes for salvation, and the great day of judgment will be delayed until he comes again.

44

is even greater than Moses because he brings a greater deliverance and (2) he has more glory because he is the Son (Heb. 3:1–6).

In light of the parallels between Moses and Jesus, it is not surprising to find references and allusions to Deuteronomy 18:15–22 in the New Testament. It is interesting that when John the Baptist denies that he is the Christ (the Messiah), he is asked whether he is the Prophet (John 1:20–21). Some people in Jesus' day may have distinguished the Messiah from the Prophet (7:40–41), but others may have identified the two together.[7] The woman at the well connects the Messiah's coming with the prophetic ministry of the disclosure of all things (4:25).[8] The New Testament confirms the identification of the Prophet with Jesus the Christ.

Jesus clearly states that the Scriptures bear witness of him (John 5:39), and specifically that Moses wrote of him (v. 46). Although no specific passage by Moses is identified in this text,[9] it is not surprising that Deuteronomy 18:15–22 would be part of this witness in light of how Jesus fits the role of the Prophet. Concepts in Deuteronomy 18:19 are alluded to in John 5. God warns the people that he will require it of them if they do not listen to the prophet who speaks in his name (Deut. 18:19). Jesus comes in the name of the Father, and the people do not receive him (John 5:43). Jesus defines his ministry as that of a *prophet* when he talks of being sent by the authority of the Father and speaking what the Father has given him to speak (12:49–50).

The key text of Deuteronomy 18:15 is cited twice in Acts. In the speech of Stephen in Acts 7, he gives a review of the history of

7. Edward J. Young, *My Servants the Prophets* (Grand Rapids: Eerdmans, 1952), 32–33. Herman N. Ridderbos shows that the prophet and the Messiah are clearly distinguished at Qumran. *The Gospel of John* (Grand Rapids: Eerdmans, 1997), 64–65.

8. D. A. Carson, *The Gospel according to John* (Grand Rapids: Eerdmans, 1991), 226. He notes that the Samaritans did not use the term *Messiah* but preferred the term *Taheb*, which may mean "the Restorer." This One would reveal the truth in line with his role as the ultimate Prophet.

9. Ibid. Carson notes that this is referring to a certain way of reading the Scriptures rather than to specific passages.

CHRIST AS PROPHET: MIGHTY IN WORD AND DEED

Israel to answer the charge that he spoke against the temple and the law. Part of his argument is that the Jewish people's refusal to acknowledge Jesus as the Messiah lines up with their treatment of God's messengers in the Old Testament. Moses was rejected by the people of Israel, the same Moses who spoke the words of Deuteronomy 18:15. Since the point of his sermon is that the current generation has betrayed and murdered Jesus (Acts 7:52), it seems clear that the citation of Deuteronomy is meant to speak of Jesus.[10]

In Acts 3:22 Peter cites Deuteronomy in a sermon to explain the significance of his healing of the lame beggar. The man was healed by the power of Jesus, whom God glorified after his death (vv. 11–16). Although the people acted in ignorance, the death of Jesus was foretold by the prophets. The people must now repent so that their sins would be blotted out and times of refreshing would be poured on them by God. Such blessing would include the consummation of all things by the coming of Christ, which the prophets also foretold (vv. 17–21).[11] Peter demonstrates that the prophets spoke of these events in two ways. He confirms that Moses spoke of the day of Christ when he cites Deuteronomy 18. Not only is the singular for *prophet* used, but a single individual is highlighted with the use of *that prophet* to whom the people must listen (Acts 3:22–23).[12] The prophets who came after Moses also proclaimed the days of Christ (v. 24).

A Prophet Mighty in Word

During his earthly ministry Jesus was mighty in his use of the Word of God. Just after his baptism he was led by the Spirit into the wilderness to be tempted by the devil. He met each tempta-

10. I. Howard Marshall, "Acts," in *Commentary on the New Testament Use of the Old Testament*, ed. G. K. Beale and D. A. Carson (Grand Rapids: Baker, 2007), 563.
11. F. F. Bruce, *The Book of Acts* (Grand Rapids: Eerdmans, 1977), 89–92.
12. E. W. Hengstenberg, *Christology of the Old Testament* (Grand Rapids: Kregel, 1970), 39.

tion with a reference to the Word of God. After Jesus fasted for forty days the tempter challenged him that if he was the Son of God, he should command stones to become bread (Matt. 4:3). In other words, Jesus should prove his identity by using his power to meet his need for food. Jesus cites Deuteronomy 8:3 to show that physical bread is not the only thing that matters in life; there is more important spiritual food by which human beings must live. The Word of God is the true source of life.

In the second temptation the devil takes Jesus to the pinnacle of the temple and challenges him to prove his identity by jumping so that the angels would catch him (Matt. 4:5–6). The tempter even quotes from Psalm 91:11–12 to give support for this suggestion. Jesus' response is to quote from Deuteronomy 6:16 because he realizes that such an act would be putting God to the test. He would be trying to force God to act in a certain way to prove something that did not need proving. In the third temptation Jesus is taken to a high mountain and is shown all the kingdoms of the world and their glory. The devil promises to give these to Jesus if he will worship him (Matt. 4:9). Here the temptation is for Jesus to receive in the wrong way what he has already been promised by his Father. Satan is offering these things to Jesus apart from his suffering and death on the cross. Jesus cites Deuteronomy 6:13 to show that God is the only One to be worshiped, even if that means suffering and death. Instead of entertaining the possibilities that the temptations offered, as Eve did in the garden, Jesus rejects the offers by citing Scripture.[13] Whereas Adam and Eve failed to fulfill their prophetic role of correctly handling the word of God, Jesus succeeds in using the Word of God to defeat the devil.

Jesus was also mighty in word in the authority of his teaching (Matt. 7:28–29). People were astonished because he did not teach them as their scribes taught. The teaching of the scribes

---

13. For a comparison of the temptation of Adam and Eve with the temptation of Jesus, see R. C. Sproul, *Following Christ* (Wheaton, IL: Tyndale House, 1983), 70–75.

was based on the authority of what their ancestors said, so they were constantly referencing the views of the rabbis.[14] Jesus did not base his teaching on the authority of anyone else but taught on the basis of his own authority. He had this authority because he was the Son of God. The prophets regularly used the messenger formula ("Thus saith the LORD") to demonstrate that the word they proclaimed was the word of God. Jesus does not use the messenger formula when he speaks because he is the Lord. He also prefaces statements with "Truly, truly, I say to you."[15] This statement occurs in John 1:51, where significant assertions are made concerning his identity. Nathanael calls him the Son of God and the King of Israel (v. 49). In response Jesus affirms his deity by identifying himself as the glorious Son of Man. He prefaces this statement with "Truly, truly, I say to you." The word *truly* is the word for *amen* and is often used to give one's consent to a prayer. Jesus' use of this formula to preface what he says is unique to him and grants certainty to his words.[16] He can be certain because he is the very truth of God and gives life to those who acknowledge him as the way to God.[17]

Jesus was also not afraid to speak the truth, both to the people and to the leaders. In fact, he spoke difficult things before large crowds. In Luke 11:29, when the crowds are increasing, Jesus states, "This generation is an evil generation. It seeks for a sign, but no sign will be given to it except the sign of Jonah." Great crowds accompany him, and he says, "If anyone comes to me and does not hate his own father and mother and wife and children and brothers and sisters, yes, even his own life, he cannot

14. Ridderbos, *Matthew*, 157. William Hendriksen lists six ways that Jesus' teaching differed from the scribes'. *Exposition of the Gospel according to Matthew* (Grand Rapids: Baker, 1973), 382–83.

15. The double formula *truly, truly* occurs only in John's Gospel, and it occurs often.

16. Morris, *John*, 169–70.

17. Carson, *John*, 491. He points out that Jesus is the Savior (4:42) and the Lamb of God (1:29). He is the One who, as the way to God, mediates God's truth and life so that no one comes to the Father except through him.

be my disciple" (14:25). He also says that if someone wants to be his disciple, he must count the cost and take up the cross. Jesus tells the parable of the self-righteous Pharisee because some in the crowd trusted in their own righteousness and treated others with contempt (18:9–14). Jesus also speaks words of judgment concerning the scribes and Pharisees because they fail to practice what they preach, and they pile heavy burdens on the people (Matt. 23:1–36). He also weeps over the hard-hearted rebellion of the people of Jerusalem, who killed the prophets and refused to come under Jesus' authority (vv. 37–39). They will also kill him, leading to Jerusalem's destruction.

Jesus offers salvation to those who will receive the truth and covenant judgment to those who reject it. He stands in the line of Isaiah the prophet, whose message was rejected by many, leading to hardened hearts. The words of Isaiah 6:9–10 are used by Jesus as an explanation for why he speaks to the people in parables (Matt. 13:14–15; Mark 4:11–12). Through his ministry, Isaiah's prophecy is being fulfilled. Jesus speaks the truth because words of truth will sift the people, separating out those who are not serious about being his disciples. He is also the covenant Mediator who prosecutes the covenant against those who reject the Word of God. But Jesus is greater than any of the prophets who have gone before, because he not only prosecutes the covenant but has the authority to establish a new covenant (Luke 22:20).

A Prophet Mighty in Prayer

In his earthly ministry Jesus fulfills the work of a prophet in speaking the word of God, but he also fulfills it through the ministry of prayer.[18] Luke 3:21–22 mentions that Jesus was praying at his baptism when the Holy Spirit descended on him and a

---

18. For a summary of the Lord's practice of prayer, see James Thomson, *The Praying Christ* (Grand Rapids: Eerdmans, 1959), 34–55.

voice from heaven declared that he was the beloved Son.[19] Jesus prayed all night before he chose the twelve apostles (6:12–13). It is somewhat speculative to ask what Jesus would be praying about, but he was probably praying for those whom he would choose to be his apostles. The importance of this decision is seen in the amount of time he spent praying beforehand. In another instance, after a busy day of healing people with various ailments, he arose early the next morning and went to a desolate place to pray (Mark 1:35). Luke 5:16 mentions that as the report about Jesus spread and great crowds gathered to hear him and to be healed, he would withdraw to desolate places to pray. Times of prayer must have been a normal part of Jesus' life and ministry, including times of prolonged prayer.[20] Jesus was praying when he asked the disciples about who the crowds thought he was (9:18). After Jesus fed the five thousand and before he walked on the Sea of Galilee, he went up on the mountain to pray (Matt. 14:23; Mark 6:46). Jesus also took Peter, James, and John up the mountain to pray, and while he was praying he was transfigured before them (Luke 9:28–29).

Jesus also prayed fervently in the garden of Gethsemane concerning the cup that he was about to drink. The agony of his troubled soul is seen in these ways: (1) he said that his soul was sorrowful even to death (Mark 14:34), (2) he fell to the ground to pray (Matt. 26:39), (3) he had three sessions of prayer (vv. 38–45), and (4) his sweat became like great drops of blood (Luke 22:44).[21] This fits the picture of Jesus in Hebrews 5:7: "In the days of his

19. David Crump, *Jesus the Intercessor: Prayer and Christology in Luke–Acts* (Grand Rapids: Baker, 1992), 24–25. He shows that Jesus' intercessory role is rooted in his filial relationship with the Father; in other words, his role as Son of God—not his subsequent role as risen Lord—is the basis of his intercessory role, which begins in his earthly ministry and continues in his exaltation to the right hand of the Father.

20. For a discussion of how Jesus' prayer life conformed to the Jewish practice of praying three times a day (sunrise, afternoon, and sunset) and how his prolonged times of prayer at night differed from the Jewish practice, see Joachin Jeremias, *The Prayers of Jesus* (London: SCM Press, 1967), 66–77.

21. Sweating drops of blood is associated with a physical condition called hematidrosis, in which the strain from extreme anguish results in the dilating of subcutaneous

flesh, Jesus offered up prayers and supplications, with loud cries and tears, to him who was able to save him from death." That Jesus wrestled with his Father in prayer is a testimony to his true humanity and stands him in a long line of saints (lament psalms) and prophets (Habakkuk, Jeremiah) who also wrestled with God.[22] Jesus' ministry of prayer included praying for his disciples (Luke 22:31–32; John 17:9, 20), praying for the people (Luke 23:34),[23] and teaching others how to pray (Matt. 6:5–15; Luke 11:1). Thus prayer becomes one of the means by which Jesus fulfills his messianic ministry.[24] The Word of God and prayer were at the heart of Jesus' ministry as a Prophet and will be important for defining the work of the apostles and elders of the church.

A Prophet Mighty in Suffering

That Jesus must depend on his Father in heaven and wrestle with him in prayer is a reminder of the suffering of the prophets in the Old Testament. Like the prophets of old, Jesus is willing to suffer for the truth that he speaks. In many ways Jeremiah represents a foreshadowing of the suffering that Jesus would experience. Both preached a message of destruction (Jer. 1:10; Matt. 11:20–24) and salvation (Jer. 1:10; Matt. 9:1–8). Both preached judgment against the people and their false expectations (Jer. 7:1–4; John 6:52–71), and both confronted the leaders of the people (Jer. 37; Matt. 23). Both were rejected by close friends and family. Jeremiah was denounced by friends (Jer. 20:10) and the people of

---

capillaries until they burst. William Hendriksen, *Exposition of the Gospel according to Luke* (Grand Rapids: Baker, 1978), 983.

22. Although Jesus was fully God, he was also a human being dependent on the Father, which is demonstrated in his life of prayer. Thomson, *The Praying Christ*, 34, 53.

23. Ibid., 50–51. Thomson argues that while on the cross Jesus prays for forgiveness for both the Roman soldiers and the Jewish people (Luke 23:34).

24. Crump, *Jesus the Intercessor*, 142–44. He also comments that Luke presents Jesus as the final Prophet, the Son of God and Messiah, who pursues the ministry of teaching and healing through God's power available through prayer (136).

his hometown (11:21). At one point in Jesus' ministry his family thought he was out of his mind (Mark 3:21). They mistook his zeal for God and God's work as madness.[25] Jesus was rejected by the people of his hometown of Nazareth when he taught in their synagogue. Although they were astonished at his wisdom and mighty works, Jesus was too familiar for them to acknowledge who he was, so they took offense at him (Matt. 13:53–58). Their unbelief was the reason he could not do many mighty works there. Jesus offers his perspective on the situation with a proverb: "A prophet is not without honor except in his hometown and in his own household" (v. 57). He affirms that he is a Prophet in explaining why he did not do many miracles in his hometown when he had done many miracles elsewhere.

Jeremiah was opposed by the people (Jer. 26:7), the priests (20:1), the prophets (28:1–16), and the kings (22:1–30). Jesus' message was opposed by the throngs of Jerusalem (Luke 23:18–25), the Pharisees (Matt. 22:15–22), the scribes (Mark 11:18), the Sadducees (Matt. 22:23–33), and the high priest (26:57–68). Jeremiah and Jesus' message was a threat to the leaders of God's people. Jesus was also betrayed by one of his own disciples (v. 14). Like Jeremiah, Jesus also wrestled with God's will for his life (vv. 36–46). Jeremiah could even write that he was like a lamb led to the slaughter (Jer. 11:19). But Jesus' ministry is different from Jeremiah's and from the ministry of every other prophet. Although Jeremiah did not give his life in fulfilling the role of a prophet, there were Old Testament prophets who did die (Jer. 26:19–23). Jesus also died, but his death was unlike the death of any other prophet. Jesus' suffering culminated in the cross, where he continued to speak the word of God's judgment (Luke 23:28–31) and salvation (v. 43), which were accomplished through his death.

25. There is debate whether Mark 3:21 is referring to Jesus' family or his friends. Although William L. Lane translates the Greek phrase as *friends*, he discusses this text under the broader heading of "The Character of Jesus' Family." *The Gospel according to Mark* (Grand Rapids: Eerdmans, 1974), 138.

A Prophet Mighty in Deed

The two men on the road to Emmaus also declared that Jesus of Nazareth was a Prophet mighty in deed before God and all the people (Luke 24:19). When Jesus raised a widow's son from the dead, fear seized the people; they glorified God and proclaimed that a great Prophet had arisen among them (7:16). The connection of mighty deeds with a great prophet is not unusual in light of the ministry of several prophets of old who performed great wonders. Moses was used by God to deliver his people from slavery in Egypt through the plagues. This deliverance was more than just a sociological deliverance of Israel from slavery. It was a spiritual battle that resulted in a spiritual victory of Yahweh over Pharaoh and the gods of Egypt (Ex. 7:4–5; 12:12). A serpent on Pharaoh's crown was believed to give Pharaoh power from the gods.[26] He represented the power of the serpent so that slavery was not just a physical bondage but a spiritual bondage. God displayed his power over the spiritual forces of darkness by the plagues, which led to the deliverance of God's people. On the Mount of Transfiguration Jesus spoke with two great prophets of his own "exodus," which he would accomplish in Jerusalem (Luke 9:31). Although Moses may have represented the Law and Elijah the Prophets, both of which Jesus had come to fulfill,[27] the mention of Jesus' departure with the use of the word *exodus* would remind readers of that great redemptive event of the Old Testament.

Jesus also came to do battle with the spiritual forces of evil. He demonstrated his power over the kingdom of darkness by casting out demons. When he is accused of casting out demons by the power of Satan (Luke 11:15), he responds that if Satan is so divided against himself, his kingdom would not

---

26. John D. Currid, *Ancient Egypt and the Old Testament* (Grand Rapids: Baker, 1997), 91.

27. Hendriksen, *Luke*, 505.

stand. Instead, someone stronger than Satan is here, One who has power over the demons. Jesus alludes to the plagues when he states that if he casts out demons by the finger of God, the kingdom of God is among them (v. 20). The phrase *finger of God* was used by the Egyptian magicians when they could not replicate the third plague (Ex. 8:19). Jesus has come to do battle with the serpent to deliver his people from the power of evil. He casts out many demons, and even the demons recognize who he is. In Luke 4:34 an unclean demon cries out, "What have you to do with us, Jesus of Nazareth? Have you come to destroy us? I know who you are—the Holy One of God." This is an exclamation of terror and dismay; the demon knows that destruction is awaiting him from One more powerful than he is.[28] Jesus will bring a greater deliverance than Moses in the complete destruction of the forces of evil when the kingdom of God triumphs (Col. 2:15).

Although Elijah's ministry is associated with John the Baptist, general associations can be made between Elijah and Jesus concerning the great deeds that a prophet is able to accomplish. Just as Elijah demonstrated power over the natural element of rain (1 Kings 17:1), raised the widow's son from the dead (vv. 17–24), and defeated the prophets of Baal on Mount Carmel (ch. 18), so Jesus demonstrated power over the storm on the sea (Luke 8:22–25), defeated the power of darkness by setting free a man possessed by many demons (vv. 26–39), and raised Jairus's daughter from the dead (vv. 40–43, 49–56). But Elisha, who followed Elijah and received a double portion of his spirit, performed more miracles than Elijah did. Many of those miracles foreshadowed the miracles of Jesus. In fact, when John the Baptist hears from prison about the deeds of Christ, he sends his disciples to ask Jesus whether he is really the One

28. Norval Geldenhuys, *Commentary on the Gospel of Luke* (Grand Rapids: Eerdmans, 1977), 173.

who is to come or whether they should look for another. Jesus responds by highlighting the good news of his ministry and its deeds of salvation that parallel Elisha's ministry: the blind receive their sight (2 Kings 6:18–20); lepers are cleansed (5:1–14); the dead are raised up (4:32–37); and the poor have good news preached to them—the widow's oil (vv. 1–7), the good news that the Shunammite woman would have a child (vv. 9–17), and works of mercy toward the sons of the prophets (vv. 38–44; 6:1–7). In addition to these parallels with Elisha's ministry, it is clear that Jesus is greater than Elisha. Elisha received a double portion of Elijah's spirit, but Jesus receives the Holy Spirit without measure (John 3:34). Elisha's miracles were used by God to encourage his people and reestablish his rule in the kingdom of Israel. Jesus' miracles demonstrate God's power to save, but the kingdom that he established is greater than the Old Testament rule of God in Israel.

Jesus is a Prophet mighty in word and deed. His ministry is effective because he is not just a human prophet. He does not just proclaim the word of God; he is the Word of God who was with God from the beginning (John 1:1). He is the Creator and the giver of life (vv. 3–4). He is the Anointed One sent from God to proclaim the good news of the day of salvation (Isa. 61:1–2a; Luke 4:16–21). He is the Christ, the Messiah sent from God to proclaim the good news of the kingdom (Mark 1:1, 15). He is the light that shines in darkness, showing people the way to live: "a light for revelation to the Gentiles, and for glory to your people Israel" (Luke 2:32). Even in his humanity Jesus is full of wisdom (v. 52). As the Word become flesh (John 1:14), he is the fullness of the wisdom of God (1 Cor. 1:24; Col. 2:3). This is the source of the authority of his teaching and the power of his Word over creation, human life, and salvation itself. The wisdom of the Old Testament found in the work of the scribes and the writing of Proverbs finds its fulfillment in Jesus. He can declare, "I am the way, the truth, and the life" (John 14:6), and therefore is the only One who can reconcile a person to God the Father. Jesus accomplishes all that the Word of God has the power to accomplish. As the Word of God, Jesus has the power to revive the soul (Mark 2:1–12), make wise the simple (Matt. 13:51–52; Luke 21:15), and enlighten the eyes (John 9:39).[29]

Jesus continues his prophetic ministry following his ascension into heaven, where he gives the apostles further revelation of his Word through the Spirit.[30] Jesus continues to work in the book of Acts as the proclamation of the Word causes the church to grow and be edified. In the six summary statements in Acts, the Word of God is at the heart of the growth of the church either explicitly (6:7; 12:24; 19:20) or implicitly (9:31; 16:5; 28:31). The apostolic and prophetic Word becomes the foundation of the church (Eph. 2:20). Peter acknowledges that the prophetic Word is more sure than the voice that the disciples heard from heaven, so it is important for the church to give great attention to it (2 Peter 1:16–21). The source of the Word is God himself. The author of Hebrews recognizes the finality of the Word spoken by Jesus the Son, not only over the many times and ways in which God spoke through the prophets, but also because of Jesus' character and work (Heb. 1:1–13). When he comes again he will conquer through his Word, since he will bear the name "The Word of God," and a sharp sword will come out of his mouth to strike down the nations (Rev. 19:13–15). The Word of God will triumph because Christ is the great Prophet, but even more because he is the Son of God.

29. For a discussion of how Psalm 19:7–11 relates to Christ, see Richard P. Belcher Jr., *The Messiah and the Psalms* (Ross-shire, UK: Christian Focus, 2006), 50–55.

30. Jesus promised his disciples that the Holy Spirit would lead them into further truth (John 14:26). With the establishment of a new covenant, the expectation would have been for further written documents. Michael J. Kruger, *Canon Revisited* (Wheaton, IL: Crossway, 2012), 160–70; Michael J. Kruger, *The Question of Canon: Challenging the Status Quo in the New Testament Debate* (Downers Grove, IL: InterVarsity Press, 2013), 79–118.

Study Questions

1. Discuss John the Baptist's role in preparing the way for Jesus.
2. How is Jesus a Prophet like Moses in fulfillment of Deuteronomy 18:15?
3. Discuss the various ways that Jesus demonstrates his authority in his use of the Word of God. What are the implications of his message compared to those of other religions?
4. What role did prayer play in Jesus' earthly ministry?
5. How did Jesus' suffering reflect the life of a prophet?
6. How does Jesus' ministry relate to the ministries of Elijah and Elisha?

4

THE ROLE OF THE PRIEST
IN THE OLD TESTAMENT

BEFORE PRIESTLY DUTIES are described in the Mosaic law, not much is known about the priests' specific functions. Adam's priestly role is indirectly seen through the garden of Eden's being a special place of God's presence, through the general parallels between the garden and the later tabernacle and temple, and through the two verbs used in Genesis 2:15 to describe Adam's work (see chapter 1). A mediator was not needed between God and the human beings he had created. But the entrance of sin into the world changed the relationship between God and humanity. That God must clothe Adam and Eve with animal skins alludes to the need for the shedding of blood to cover sin and shame. Altars must be built and sacrifices offered. Noah offered burnt offerings to the Lord after the flood, and Abraham built altars in Canaan as he traveled throughout the land. Job acted as a priest for his family by offering sacrifices to consecrate his children. The need for an official priesthood arose when the family of Israel grew to the size of a nation and altars became a part of sanctuaries.[1] Members of the priesthood were set apart so that they could fulfill the role of mediators between God and the people.

The role of the prophet in Israel is defined by one major text (Deut. 18:15–22), but that is not the case with the role of the priests. No one text defines their function. Their role can be ascertained from texts that (1) speak about the priestly garments (Ex. 28–29; Lev. 8–9), (2) describe the sacrifices that are brought to the Lord (chs. 1–7), (3) show the disobedience of two sons of Aaron (ch. 10), (4) give an account of the Levites' role in the movement of the tabernacle (Num. 2–4), and (5) describe the priestly benediction (6:22–27). It is also significant that Hebrews 5:1–5 gives a general description of priestly duties when comparing the works of the Old Testament high priest and Christ.

Holy Mediators

The priests fulfilled the important role of mediator between God and the people. This role included representing God to the people, but it also included bringing the needs of the people to God. The general work of the priests can be described as "ministering before the LORD" (1 Sam. 2:18). To accomplish the role of mediator, they had to be set apart as holy to the Lord. *Holiness* means to be set apart in a special way to fulfill a special function for God and his people. The priests were set apart by the garments they wore, the oil with which they were anointed, and the hereditary priestly line. It becomes apparent that even among the priests there are levels of holiness, so it is helpful to distinguish between the high priest, the priests, and the Levites.

1. Tremper Longman III, *Immanuel in Our Place* (Phillipsburg, NJ: P&R Publishing, 2001), 120.

The Priestly Line

In Exodus 28:1 Moses is told to set apart his brother Aaron and Aaron's sons to serve as priests. The priesthood is hereditary and will thus come from the descendants of Aaron. No reason is given for the choice of Aaron, but he had held a prominent role since Moses was called to deliver the people from Egypt (4:14–16). Aaron was Moses' constant companion during the plagues (11:10), the exodus (12:43), the journey to Mount Sinai (16:2), the stay at Mount Sinai when Aaron was with Moses on the mount (19:24), and the confirmation of the covenant (24:1). Sadly, he also helped the people fashion the golden calf while Moses was on the mountain receiving the law of God (ch. 32). The first mention of Aaron after this event is a passing reference that he and all the people saw the shining face of Moses when he came down with the tablets of the law after the covenant renewal with God (34:30). It is assumed that Aaron is the priest when the tabernacle and the garments for the priests are made in Exodus 35–40. Because of his role in crafting the golden calf (32:1–8) and his weak excuse when confronted by Moses (vv. 21–25), it is surprising that Aaron does not receive more condemnation or suffer more consequences for his actions. Some have tried to explain his actions as motivated by fear, which is reflected in the Peshitta,[2] and argue that he took the blame for what happened.[3] In fact, Aaron blamed the people (v. 22) instead of taking responsibility for letting them "break loose" (v. 25).

God's quick reaction of judgment to the disobedience of Aaron's sons Nadab and Abihu (Lev. 10) is different from his reaction to Aaron's disobedience in Exodus 32. This difference can be explained by the fact that Aaron and his sons had just

2. The Peshitta is the Syriac translation of the Bible. The Pentateuch was probably translated in the first century A.D.
3. Walter C. Kaiser Jr., "Exodus," in *The Expositor's Bible Commentary*, ed. Tremper Longman III and David Garland (Grand Rapids: Zondervan, 2008), 1:540.

been ordained to the priesthood in Leviticus 8–9 and that the disobedience occurred in the tabernacle. Aaron had not yet been ordained in Exodus 32. His disobedience to God did not take away his future role as priest because of God's grace. Aaron is included with the people for whom Moses interceded in Exodus 32:11–14, and he is specifically named with all the people who saw the shining face of Moses in Exodus 34:29–34 after the renewal of the covenant. They are allowed to come near to Moses, who had been in the presence of God, which is evidence that God's presence would continue to be with the people. Almost immediately instructions are given for the construction of the tabernacle and the making of the priestly garments.

Garments

The garments that the priests wore were special and distinct. Just by wearing them the priests would have stood out among the people of Israel, much as a uniform causes a police officer to stand out in a crowd. In Exodus 25–31 instructions are given to Moses concerning the building of the tabernacle, the garments of the priests, and the setting apart of the priests for service at the tabernacle. The instructions for making the priestly garments are given in chapter 28, and the making of the garments is described in chapter 39. Aaron as the high priest and his sons as priests have several things in common. They are presented together to serve the Lord (28:1). Their garments are called holy garments (v. 4), setting them apart from other Israelites so that they could fulfill their special role.[4] All the priests are to wear linen undergarments to cover their naked flesh. These undergarments reach from the hips to the thighs and are to be worn when the priests go into the Tent of Meeting or when they come near the altar to minister in the Holy Place. If they do not wear these garments, they will bear

---

4. Ibid., 1:525.

guilt and die (vv. 42–43). These instructions correspond to what God tells the Israelites concerning building the altars. If they build an altar, they will not make the altar with steps because they expose their nakedness when they step up to it (20:26). Covering their nakedness may be a reminder of the shame that comes with sin. When Adam and Eve sinned, they understood that they were naked and that they needed to be covered by God to hide their shame. The priests recognize this fact by properly covering themselves so as not to be exposed. If they ignore God's instructions, they are disobeying God, and they are also rejecting their need to be covered by God, which is a denial of their sin and its resulting shame. They become guilty and bear the punishment of death.

The garments for Aaron and his sons are also said to be "for glory and for beauty" (Ex. 28:2, 40). This description refers to the dignity and honor given to the priests.[5] It is significant that the words *kavod* (כבוד) and *tiferet* (תפארת) are also used to refer to the glory of God. The word *kavod* is the common word for God's glory, and it is used of the cloud cover at Mount Sinai, where the appearance of his glory was like a devouring fire (24:16–17). In Isaiah 63:15 heaven is the habitation of God's holiness and glory (*tiferet*), which is also manifested to his people (vv. 12–14).[6] The garments of the priests allow them to reflect the honor and glory of God to the people as they represent his presence.

The outer garments for the sons of Aaron are coats, sashes, and caps (Ex. 28:40). These are the clothing of the ordinary priests[7] and are not as elaborate as the garments of the high priest described in chapter 28. The ordinary priest will wear a coat over the linen undergarments. The word for *coat* seems to refer to an outer garment that can be seen by others. This is the word used for the covering of animal skins that God made

5. Ibid., 1:528.
6. C. John Collins, פאר, in *NIDOTTE*, 3:573–74. The marginal reading for Isaiah 63:15 says "your holy and glorious habitation."
7. Kaiser, "Exodus," 1:528.

for Adam and Eve (Gen. 3:21), for the special garment that Jacob gave to Joseph as his favored son (37:3), and for the garment with sleeves that the virgin daughters of the king wore (2 Sam. 13:18). The word is translated "robe" in Genesis 37:3 and 2 Samuel 13:18. A sash or belt would be useful if the garment was long and flowing. The cap would be another way in which the priests were set apart from other Israelites.

The garments that Aaron will wear as the high priest are also described in Exodus 28.[8] The list of garments is given in verse 4: a breastpiece, an ephod, a robe, a coat of checker work, a turban, and a sash. The garments are to be made of gold, blue and purple and scarlet yarns, and fine twined linen (v. 5). These are the same colors and materials that are used to make the curtains (26:1), showing how closely the work of the high priest is associated with the tabernacle. If the tabernacle represents the presence of God with his people, the high priest also represents the presence of God by the garments he wore and the work that he did.[9]

The garments of the high priest also highlight his role in representing the people to God. The first item described is the ephod (Ex. 28:6–14) that was worn over the robe.[10] The ephod was like an apron hung from the shoulders with two shoulder straps, which had two onyx stones attached to them. These stones contained the names of the sons of Israel, with six names

8. For a discussion of how the high priestly garments of Aaron differ from the garments of the priests in both the material used and the type of workmanship, see Menahem Haran, *Temples and Temple-Service in Ancient Israel* (Winona Lake, IN: Eisenbrauns, 1985), 171. The different types of workmanship are described on page 160.

9. Vern S. Poythress, *The Shadow of Christ in the Law of Moses* (Phillipsburg, NJ: Presbyterian and Reformed, 1991), 53. He comments that the high priest was a kind of vertical replica of the tabernacle.

10. The Hebrew word for *robe* (מעיל) in Exodus 28:31 is different from the word for *coat* (כתנת). The high priest's coat is described in verse 39, and it is different from the priest's coat (v. 40) in its description as a "checker work of fine linen." The high priest would wear linen undergarments (v. 42), a coat, a robe over the coat, and an ephod over the robe. For a visual picture of the garments of the high priest, see the *ESV Study Bible* (Wheaton, IL: Crossway, 2008), 208.

engraved on each. The setting of each stone was made of delicate patterns of gold (gold filigree) attached by two golden chains.[11] The purpose of these stones was for Aaron to bear the names of Israel before the Lord for "remembrance." God did not need to be reminded of his people because he had forgotten them, but the idea was that the high priest presented them to the God who was able to meet all their needs in light of his covenant promises. The high priest represented all Israel by presenting the people before the Lord.[12]

The breastpiece of judgment is described in Exodus 28:15–30. This garment is made in the style of the ephod with gold, blue and purple and scarlet yarns, and fine twined linen (v. 15). It is smaller than the ephod, is square, and fits over the breast of the high priest. It is folded over to form a pouch into which the UT are placed[13] and attached to the ephod by blue lace, which binds the breastpiece to the ephod through rings (vv. 22–28). On the breastpiece are twelve stones arranged in four rows of three, with the names of the sons of Israel on the stones. These represent the twelve tribes (vv. 17–21). The purpose of the twelve stones on the breastpiece is virtually identical to the purpose of the two onyx stones on the ephod: to bear the names of the sons of Israel before the Lord for remembrance (vv. 12, 29). The differences between the two, however, are significant. The ephod has two onyx stones with six names on each. The breastpiece has twelve stones, with the name of one tribe on each stone. The two onyx stones are on Aaron's shoulders (v. 12), and the twelve stones are on his heart (v. 30). The high

11. The gold thread was cut from hammered gold sheets, which gave the ephod a dazzling appearance and a rigid construction, which may have allowed it to be stored in an upright position. Cornelius Van Dam, "Priestly Clothing," in *Dictionary of the Old Testament Pentateuch*, ed. T. Desmond Alexander and David W. Baker (Downers Grove, IL: InterVarsity Press, 2003), 643.

12. John D. Currid, *A Study Commentary on Exodus*, vol. 2, *Chapters 19–40* (Darlington, UK: Evangelical Press, 2001), 197.

13. Kaiser, "Exodus," 1:527.

priest is to keep the concerns of the people of God close to his heart as he enters into God's presence. His concern is not just for the nation as a whole, but for each tribe represented. Aaron brings the concerns of the people before the Lord in order for judgment or decisions to be made on their behalf. This is the role of the UT, which is also on the heart of Aaron so that he regularly bears the judgment of the people of Israel before the Lord.[14] This demonstrates that God also cares about the concerns and decisions faced by his people and that he is ready to render decisions and act on their behalf.

The next item described is the robe that the high priest will wear (Ex. 28:31–35). It is called the "robe of the ephod" because it is worn under the ephod. The robe is a blue, whole garment that slips over the head. The hem contains pomegranates of blue, purple, and scarlet yarns interspaced with golden bells. Aaron must wear the robe so that the bells will be heard when he goes in and out of the presence of the Lord in the Holy Place; otherwise, he will die. The pomegranate is one of the fruits that the spies brought back from Canaan. The priest's wearing a garment with fruit attached may signify fruitfulness.[15] The work of the high priest will be fruitful as he ministers in obedience to the God who is the source of the people's fruitfulness. The bells that the high priest wears on the hem of the robe may highlight his dangerous work and the possibility of his death when coming before the Lord. Although the text does not specifically state the purpose of the bells, it is dangerous to enter the presence of the king unannounced, so perhaps the sound of the bells announces the approach of the high priest.[16] From the perspective of those outside the Holy Place, the sound of the bells lets people know that the priest is alive and is ministering on their behalf.[17] The

14. For a discussion of the role of the UT, see chapter 2.
15. Currid, *Exodus*, 205.
16. Ibid., 206.
17. Kaiser, "Exodus," 1:528.

people are also reminded that God must be approached on his terms, not theirs.[18]

The turban that the high priest wore is described in Exodus 28:36–38. A plate of pure gold engraved with the words "Holy to the LORD" is attached to it. Wearing the turban is associated with the high priest's role as mediator between the holiness of the Lord and the sinfulness of the people. Aaron presents the people before the Lord by bearing "any guilt from the holy things that the people of Israel consecrate as their holy gifts" (v. 38). When the people consecrate their sacrifices, the priest can carry away their guilt in the name of God.[19] The bearing of guilt in Leviticus 10:17 is related to making atonement for the people. The sacrifices that the priests offer for the people will take away their sin. In this way the people are "accepted before the LORD" (Ex. 28:38).

Consecrated for Service: Anointed with Oil

Aaron and his sons are set apart as priests, and all future priests must come from Aaron's line. Making the priesthood hereditary set it apart, because not just any Israelite could become a priest. Aaron is from the tribe of Levi; he and his sons Nadab, Abihu, Eleazar, and Ithamar (Ex. 6:16, 23) are all consecrated as priests in a special ceremony. The instructions for this ceremony (28:41) are expanded in chapter 29 and implemented in Leviticus 8.

The instructions in Exodus 28:41 specify that Moses is to put the garments on Aaron and his sons, anoint (*mashakh*, מָשַׁח) them, ordain them (literally, "fill their hand"), and consecrate (*qadash*, קְדַשׁ) them to serve God as priests (Ex. 28; Lev. 8). First, Aaron and his sons are brought to the entrance of the Tent of Meeting and washed with water (Lev. 8:6). This shows their need

---

18. John N. Oswalt, "Exodus," in *Cornerstone Biblical Commentary*, ed. Philip W. Comfort (Carol Stream, IL: Tyndale House, 2008), 1:509.

19. Ibid., 1:507, 1:509.

for purification before they put on the priestly garments. Then the garments of the priesthood are placed on them, with the high priestly garments placed on Aaron (Ex. 28:6–39) and the regular priestly garments placed on his sons (v. 41). The anointing oil is used to set apart the tabernacle, specifically the altar, its utensils, the basin, and its stand (Lev. 8:10–13). Then anointing oil is poured on Aaron's head. The focus on Aaron highlights his special duties as high priest and signifies the positive inauguration and dedication of someone for special service. Anointing with oil conveyed a special status of holiness for that person, empowering him to carry out his role. This empowerment comes through spiritual endowment as anointing with oil becomes associated with the Holy Spirit (Isa. 61:1; Zech. 4:1–14).[20]

Several sacrifices are offered on behalf of Aaron and his sons (Lev. 8:14–21). The bull of the sin offering is slaughtered as they place their hands on its head. Placing one's hands on the head of the sacrificial animal identified a person with the animal's death, recognizing that the animal must die in the person's place (substitutionary atonement). Aaron and his sons need the blood of a sacrifice to cover their sins. But the altar also needs to be set apart for its special use, so Moses takes blood to purify the altar and to make atonement for it. When the verb *to make atonement* is used with an inanimate object, the idea is to wipe clean or purge (expiation).[21] The blood of the bull of the sin offering sets the altar apart for its special use in the tabernacle. Next the ram of the burnt offering is sacrificed. Aaron and his sons again lay their hands on the head of the sacrificial animal. This offering is wholly consumed on the altar as a pleasing aroma to God. It is accepted by him, and this means that the one bringing the offering

20. Ibid., 1:510–11; John N. Oswalt, משׁח, *NIDOTTE*, 2:1124–26. The concept *Messiah* or *Anointed One* (*mashiakh*) comes from the verb *to anoint* (*mashakh*).
21. Richard E. Averbeck, כפר, *NIDOTTE*, 2:696.

is accepted by him. The priests need the sacrifices for their own sin before they can offer sacrifices for the sin of others.

The next sacrifice is unique to the ordination service (Lev. 8:22–29). The ram of ordination is sacrificed as Aaron and his sons lay their hands on its head. The blood of the sacrifice is not put on the horns of the altar or thrown against its sides; it is put on the right earlobes, the right thumbs, and the right big toes of Aaron and his sons. The right side denotes strength, and this action signifies that they are totally committed in every part of their life to do the work of priests. They are ready to listen to God, to do God's work, and to walk in God's ways.[22] The word *ordination* literally means "filling" and is short for "to fill the hand" (in verse 33 the full phrase is used). This refers to taking some of the sacrificial animal, along with unleavened bread and oil, and putting them into the hands of Aaron and his sons. These items are then waved before the Lord as a wave offering[23] before being burned on the altar. This signifies that Aaron and his sons are empowered to do the work of priests and have a right to receive priests' benefits for their work, namely, a portion of certain offerings.[24] In the ordination service the portion of the animal normally given to the priest is given back to God as a wave offering. Everything about the life and work of the priest is done in honor of God.

The ceremony ends with a covenant meal, which Aaron and his sons eat together at the entrance of the tabernacle (Lev. 8:31–36). The meal celebrates the bond established between God and the priesthood. The priests are to remain at the entrance of the tabernacle for seven days to repeat the sacrifices each

22. John D. Currid, *A Study Commentary on Leviticus* (Darlington, UK: Evangelical Press, 2004), 108.
23. Ibid., 98. It is unclear what action is signified by the wave offering. There may have been some movement back and forth over the altar or the elevation of the offering over the altar.
24. Ibid., 108–9.

day. This means that the consecration is complete and that full atonement is made for Aaron and his sons. They are not to enter the tabernacle before the service is complete, and they are not to abandon their calling by leaving the tabernacle area. The account ends with a statement of the obedience of Aaron and his sons to all that the Lord commanded them.

The Ministry of the Levites

The significant role of the Levites is important in light of their history. Simeon and Levi, sons of Jacob, were cursed by their father for deceit, anger, and revenge over the defilement of their sister Dinah (Gen. 49:5–7). The curse was that they would be divided and scattered in Israel. Historically, Simeon was the smallest tribe in the census of Numbers 26. This tribe received land in the desert region in the vicinity of Judah and became integrated into the tribe of Judah (Josh. 19:1, 9). The descendants of Levi did not receive an inheritance of land and were scattered among the other tribes. But the curse of being scattered was turned into a blessing because the sons of Levi supported Moses in the golden-calf incident (Ex. 32:28–29). They went throughout the camp of Israel and put to death those who were participating in idolatry. Moses blessed them by setting them apart for the service of the Lord to assist the priests in their work. When Moses blessed the Levites, he used the same terminology that had been used in the ceremony to set apart Aaron and his sons. The Levites were "ordained for the service of the Lord." The word *ordained* is a translation of the phrase "fill their hand." Although the duties of the Levites were different from the duties of the priests, they enjoyed benefits from the sacrificial offerings (Deut. 18:1) and were supported by tithes (Num. 18:21). Although they did not receive land as an inheritance, they did receive forty-eight towns scattered throughout the tribes. The faithful actions of the sons of Levi turned a curse into a blessing.

The Relationship to the Firstborn

The Levites have a special relationship to the firstborn of Israel (Num. 3); they take their place (vv. 11–13). The firstborn belong to the Lord because God consecrated them to himself when he struck down the firstborn of Egypt. Thus the firstborn belonged to God, and now the Levites also belong to God. They take the place of the firstborn and are given to assist the priests (vv. 6–7).

The dedication of the Levites to serve in place of the firstborn of Israel highlights the special role of the firstborn, who might otherwise have been appointed to the task given to the Levites.[25] Before Aaron and his sons were set apart to the priesthood (Ex. 29), priests were mentioned when Israel was at Mount Sinai. Moses warned the priests who came near to consecrate themselves (19:22). Who were these priests? It is possible that the firstborn of Israel served in some capacity in a priestly role before the construction of the tabernacle.[26] They are consecrated to the Lord after the institution of the Passover and the tenth plague, which killed all the firstborn in Egypt (13:1–2). The Levites take their place as they assist in the work of the newly ordained priests.

Guarding the Tabernacle

The regulations of Numbers 1:1–10:10 help prepare Israel for military occupation of the land. Israel as the army of God (Ex. 6:26; 13:18) will be leaving Mount Sinai and moving toward Canaan. The Levites will assist the priests in helping Israel move toward the Promised Land in a way that ensures the purity of the camp (Num. 1–4). The census of chapter 1 covers all males who are at least twenty years old and who are able to go to war. The Levites are exempt from this census because of the spe-

---

25. R. Dennis Cole, *Numbers* (Nashville: Broadman & Holman, 2000), 94.
26. Kaiser, "Exodus," 1:476.

cial role that God has given them. Instead of warriors going to battle, they are in charge of moving the tabernacle. Their general duties are laid out in Numbers 1:47–54. The arrangement of the camp is laid out in chapter 2. The tabernacle is at the center, and the Levites camp around it. As Israel moves toward the land of Canaan, the Levites lead the way. The specific duties of the clans of Gershon, Merari, and Kohath in moving the tabernacle are given in chapters 3 and 4.

The tribe of Levi was presented to Aaron to assist him (Num. 3:5–10). The terms used (*bring* and *set them before*) signified their consecration to this work and their subservient ministry to the priests.[27] The phrase used to describe the work of the Levites is *keep guard* (1:53; 3:7). The tabernacle represented the presence of God and was considered to be sacred space. An Israelite could not wander into the tabernacle area without grave consequences. If an outsider came near it, he would be put to death (v. 51). An outsider was any unauthorized person, who in this case was any non-Levite.[28] The guarding of the tabernacle also meant that the Levites would camp around it to perform "guard duty," which might include putting someone to death (Ex. 32:25–29).[29] Thus they protected the purity of the holy, sacred space of God's presence in the tabernacle so that his wrath would not fall on the camp (Num. 1:53).[30]

The Levites specifically have charge of taking down the tabernacle, moving it, and then setting it up again (Num. 1:50). The duties of the different clans are given in chapters 3–4. The three sons of Levi at the head of the three branches of the Levites are Gershon, Kohath, and Merari. Numbers 3:14–20 lists them with

27. Cole, *Numbers*, 93.
28. Timothy R. Ashley, *The Book of Numbers* (Grand Rapids: Eerdmans, 1993), 68.
29. This tribe had a warlike character (Gen. 49:5–7), which was put to good use in some of their duties. Ashley (ibid., 69) points out that the same term used of the military service of the rest of the tribes (צבא) was also used of the Levites (Num. 4:23).
30. Longman, *Immanuel*, 139. He calls them God's bodyguards.

their clans, and the list is followed by a census of the Levites according to their clans, along with a statement of their specific responsibilities (vv. 21–39). Then chapter 4 gives more details on how the tabernacle is to be dismantled and moved. How the tabernacle is moved shows respect for the place of God's presence and allows the ark of the covenant to lead the people. Several important words are used for the work of the Levites. Numbers 3:7 uses the two words that are used for Adam's work in the garden of Eden (*shamar*, שָׁמַר; *avad*, אָבַד). The Levites "keep," in the sense of *guard*, and "work" in relationship to the tabernacle. The guarding aspect is emphasized in the word for *guard duty* (*mishmeret*, מִשְׁמֶרֶת), which occurs twelve times in chapters 3 and 4. Three other words are also used to describe their duties. Two of the words emphasize work. The Levites' work[31] is their occupation (4:3), which includes physical labor (*avodah*, אֲבֹדָה), such as carrying the articles, utensils, and frames of the tabernacle with its bars, pillars, and bases (v. 31). By faithfully working, they ministered to the priests (3:6). The principle lived out by the Levites is that work is a way to serve both God and other people.

Aaron and his sons are the only ones allowed to go into the Most Holy Place to prepare it for travel (Num. 4:1–15). Eleazar, son of Aaron, has oversight of the whole tabernacle (v. 16). The furniture and utensils must be covered, and then the Kohathites will carry those articles. But if the sons of Kohath look on the holy things even for a moment (v. 20) or touch them (v. 15), they will die. The work of the Kohathites is dangerous because one wrong move or glance can bring death. The other two clans carry items of the tabernacle that are not as dangerous. After the holy things have been removed, the coverings for the tent and the screens are removed by the Gershonites, leaving the

---

31. Stephen Hague comments that this word "can refer to specific work projects or to the routine of a particular business endeavor of any class of labor from menial to royal" (מְלָאכָה, *NIDOTTE*, 2:943).

framework of the tabernacle with its bars, pillars, and bases for the Merarites to move.[32]

The work of the Levites is important because it allows Israel, the army of God, to move from Mount Sinai and journey toward the Promised Land to engage in military battle (Num. 10:11–36). The ark of the covenant leads the way because God, also represented by the pillar of cloud (vv. 11, 34), is leading his people. When the ark sets out, Moses proclaims, "Arise, O LORD, let your enemies be scattered" (v. 35). This has been called the "Battle Cry of Moses"[33] and expresses joyous excitement and the hope of victory as God leads his people into battle.[34] When the ark comes to rest, Moses declares, "Return, O LORD, to the ten thousand thousands of Israel" (v. 36). When the ark stops along the journey, the Lord is present again with his people, the army of Israel.

The role of the Levites changed once the ark became housed in a stationary temple and was not moved from place to place. David instituted this change when the ark was brought to Jerusalem, before the temple was built. The Levites participated in its transportation to Jerusalem (1 Chron. 15). Some carried the ark of God on their shoulders with poles (v. 15), some played loudly on musical instruments to raise sounds of joy (v. 16), one directed the music (v. 22), some were singers (v. 19), some blew the trumpets before it (v. 24), and some were gatekeepers (v. 24).

Assistants in Worship

First Chronicles 16 describes the sacrifices that were offered when the ark came to Jerusalem, and it also records some of the Levites' permanent appointments to minister before the ark "to invoke, to thank, and to praise the LORD" (v. 4). Certain Levites

---

32. Ashley, *Numbers*, 107.
33. Ronald B. Allen, "Numbers," in *The Expositor's Bible Commentary*, ed. Tremper Longman III and David E. Garland (Grand Rapids: Zondervan, 2012), 2:183.
34. Cole, *Numbers*, 178.

had responsibilities for playing music to assist worship. Their role was to sing thanksgiving (v. 6) and to minister regularly before the Lord as each day required (v. 37). The music and songs of praise offered by the Levites accompanied the priests as they offered the required daily sacrifices to the Lord. The Levites used their gifts in the work they were given, and they served the priests and the people of God.[35]

The Ministry of the Priests

Proper Handling of the Sacrifices

One of the major roles of the priests was to assist the people in offering their sacrifices to the Lord. The five major sacrifices are described in Leviticus 1–7, with a section devoted to instructions for the priests (6:8–7:37). The priests must know the function of each sacrifice so that they will know how to treat the animal and what to do with its blood. For example, the animal brought for the burnt offering is totally consumed on the altar (1:9), but the animal brought for the fellowship offering, also called the peace offering, is divided up so that God receives a portion, the priests receive a portion, and the one who brought the sacrifice receives a portion (ch. 3). The blood of the animal is treated differently depending on the sacrifice. The blood of the burnt offering and the fellowship offering are thrown against the sides of the altar. The blood of the sin offering is treated differently depending on the person who brought it. If an anointed priest

35. The view in contemporary scholarship is that rival groups composed of the Levites, the Aaronites, the Zadokites, and the Mushites (descended from Moses) contended for the right to officiate at the altar. See Haran, *Temples*, 84–111; Joseph Blenkinsopp, *Sage, Priest, Prophet: Religious and Intellectual Leadership in Ancient Israel* (Louisville, KY: Westminster John Knox Press, 1995). For a critique of this view, see D. A. Garrett, "Levi, Levites," in *Dictionary of the Old Testament Pentateuch*, ed. T. Desmond Alexander and David W. Baker (Downers Grove, IL: InterVarsity Press, 2003), 519–22; Ashley, *Numbers*, 86–92.

brings the sacrifice, the blood is taken into the Tent of Meeting and some of it is sprinkled in front of the veil of the sanctuary (4:6). If a common person brings a sin offering, the blood is put on the horns of the altar and the rest is poured out at the base (v. 30). The role of the priest in properly handling the animal and the blood is important because of the general purposes of the sacrifices.[36]

The blood of the sacrifice, representing the life of the animal, is given to make atonement for the people (Lev. 17:11). The sacrifices specifically said to make atonement are the burnt offering, the sin offering, and the guilt offering. In each of these offerings, the one who brings it puts his or her hand on the head of the animal while it is slain. This signifies that the life of the animal is given in exchange for the life of the one who brings the sacrifice (substitutionary atonement). Both the covering of sin (expiation) and the appeasement of the wrath of a holy God (propitiation) are seen.[37] The priests are the ones who make this possible because they handle the blood of the sacrifice. If the priests do not handle the blood properly, Israel's relationship with God is in jeopardy.

The Importance of Obedience

The necessity of the obedience of the priests is highlighted in several passages in the Old Testament (Ex. 28:43; Num. 16; Mal. 1:6–2:9). The most dramatic is the death of Nadab and Abihu in Leviticus 10. Aaron and his sons are set apart as priests in chapter 8, and they begin their ministry at the tabernacle in chapter 9. God demonstrates his pleasure by causing his glory to appear to the people and by sending fire to consume the sacrifice on the altar. The people see the fire, shout, and fall on their

36. For a description of the different sacrifices, see Longman, *Immanuel*, 75–102.
37. For a biblical discussion of these ideas, see Jay Sklar, *Sin, Impurity, Sacrifice, Atonement: The Priestly Conceptions* (Sheffield, UK: Sheffield Phoenix Press, 2005).

faces (9:23–24). Then Nadab and Abihu offer unauthorized fire before the Lord. Whatever the unauthorized fire may be,[38] it is clearly something that God "had not commanded them" (10:1). They are acting on their own in disobedience to God, whose actions are immediate and swift: fire comes down and consumes them. This act of God's judgment shows the importance of the obedience of the priests. If they are not obedient, the salvation of God's people and his presence among them are in jeopardy.

Teaching the Law

After the death of Nadab and Abihu, God instructs Aaron concerning the importance of making proper distinctions in the priests' work. The priests are to distinguish between the holy and the common and between the clean and the unclean. These are important categories for the priests to understand so that they can make proper decisions. If something is not holy, it is common. Common things are either clean or unclean. Clean things can become holy when they are set apart. Clean things can also be made unclean if they are polluted.[39] It is important that the priests make these distinctions, but also that they teach the people to make them (Lev. 10:11). In the food laws of chapter 11, these distinctions affect the people's everyday life in the food they eat.

An example of the importance of the priests' teaching the people comes from Malachi 2:1–9. This text occurs in a longer passage dealing with the priests (1:6–2:9). They were dishonoring God by allowing blemished animals to be brought as sacrifices

---

38. Suggestions include that (1) they did not take the coals in their censers from the altar of burnt offering, (2) the incense they used was not properly mixed (Ex. 30:34–38), (3) they were doing something that only the high priest was allowed to do, and (4) they were intoxicated (Lev. 10:9). The most likely option is the first because fire is the main concern of the violation. Mark F. Rooker, *Leviticus* (Nashville: Broadman & Holman, 2000), 157.

39. Gordon J. Wenham, *The Book of Leviticus* (Grand Rapids: Eerdmans, 1979), 19.

(1:7–8). These sacrifices profaned the altar of the Lord and were not acceptable to him (v. 12). If the priests did not change their ways, they would experience the judgment of God (2:2–3). He addressed the priests this way so that his covenant with Levi would stand (v. 4). Scripture contains little information on the establishment of the covenant with Levi, but it probably arose from the events in Exodus 32.[40] It is identified in Malachi 2:5 as a covenant of life and peace. The role of the Levitical priests leads to life and well-being among God's people. The actions of the priests in Malachi's day brought death and judgment. Levi feared God and honored his name. Such a priest lived before God and the people of God with integrity and was able to teach them. Such a priest guarded knowledge and taught the truth. The result of this teaching was that "he turned many from iniquity" (v. 6). Proper teaching by the priests kept God's people from living lives that were displeasing to him. Priests who were disobedient and did not teach people the truth of the law caused people to live in disobedience and jeopardize their relationship with God.

The teaching role of the priest is rooted in the fact that he is a messenger of the Lord sent to mediate the message of God's law to the people (Mal. 2:7). The term *messenger* is used for prophets and priests, and it shows similarities between the proclamation of the prophet and the teaching of the priest; yet there are differences. The prophets mediate the word (*davar*, דבר) of God

---

40. Pieter A. Verhoef, *The Books of Haggai and Malachi* (Grand Rapids: Eerdmans, 1987), 245. The connection of the covenant of Levi with Exodus 32 is that Moses uses the phrase "fill their hands" to refer to Levites' being "ordained" for the service of the Lord (v. 29). Numbers also mentions the covenant of salt in connection with the offerings for priests and Levites (ch. 18) and the covenant of peace established with Phinehas, son of Aaron (25:1–13). These two passages assume the covenant of Levi and specify the role of the priests and Levites. Numbers 18:19 confirms the work of the priests after Korah's rebellion. Ashley (*Numbers*, 337) argues that this passage redefines their role so that only they would suffer death if an Israelite trespassed against the sanctuary. Phinehas is rewarded for his actions at Baal of Peor with the promise that his descendants would have a covenant of perpetual priesthood (Num. 25:11–13). This promise establishes that the high priest would come from the descendants of Phinehas (Ashley, *Numbers*, 523).

and the priests teach the law (*torah*, תורה) of God.[41] These two overlap because they are both rooted in the revelation of God to his people in the Mosaic covenant. The proclamation of the prophets, however, is broader than the teaching of the priests. The prophets deal with the covenant life of the nation before God, and they also receive direct revelation. The priests focus on the sacrifices brought by the people and the rituals that bring the people into a state of cleanness before God (Lev. 1–15). The priest's instruction occurs in the fulfillment of his priestly role.[42]

Blessing the People of God

The priest's role as mediator between God and the people has two aspects. The priest represents the people to God by presenting their sacrifices and by interceding for them (see below). The priest also represents God to the people. The priestly blessing, found in Numbers 6:22–27, pronounces God's blessing on the people. His blessing is not limited to one aspect of life but includes its fullness. The form of the blessing shows this as the verses get progressively longer, giving the impression of a stream of blessing.[43] The word *bless* (*barakh*) in the opening line, "The LORD bless you," relates to the power to be fertile and prosperous. The closing word *peace* (*shalom*) refers to wholeness in all areas of life.[44] Such material blessing comes only because of the presence of the Lord. The middle lines of the blessing emphasize God's presence in the phrases "make his face to shine upon" (v. 25) and "lift up his countenance" (v. 26). These expressions focus on God's favor toward his people. The explanation in verse 27 emphasizes that through the pronouncement of blessing, the

41. Verhoef, *Haggai and Malachi*, 250. He comments that this distinction is also found in Jeremiah 18:18, Ezekiel 7:26, and Micah 3:11.
42. Ibid., 258.
43. Ashley, *Numbers*, 151.
44. Ibid., 151–53.

name of God is put on the people. This action sets them apart not only to receive his blessing but also to be a blessing to others as they live out what God has granted to them.

Stricter Regulations for the High Priest

The tabernacle and the priesthood have levels of holiness. The Israelites can come to the entrance of the Tent of Meeting and the priests can go into the Holy Place, but only the high priest could go into the Most Holy Place once a year. These levels of holiness are seen in the laws in the book of Leviticus. Regulations of holiness for the people are given in Leviticus 17–20. Regulations of stricter holiness in the areas of mourning and marriage practices are given for the priests and the high priest (ch. 21). Touching a dead body brought one into a state of uncleanness. The priests can touch the dead bodies only of very close relatives: mother, father, son, daughter, brother, and unmarried sister (v. 3). They are also forbidden to participate in certain mourning rites that may have been associated with pagans (v. 5).[45] The high priest is more restricted; he cannot make himself unclean for even his father or his mother (v. 11). There are also stricter regulations concerning marriage for the priests and the high priest. These regulations are important because the priesthood is hereditary. A priest cannot marry a prostitute, a woman who has been defiled, or a divorced woman (v. 7), but he can marry the widow of a priest (Ezek. 44:22). The high priest can marry only a virgin.[46] The priests are to put their priestly duties above their family ties and responsibilities.[47]

45. Rooker, *Leviticus*, 273. He comments that the prohibition of the priesthood to be involved in funerary activities was to avoid sanctioning the cults of the dead. The high priest was also not able to participate in normal mourning rites on the basis of Leviticus 21:10 (Wenham, *Leviticus*, 291). The laws regarding contact with a corpse are covered in Numbers 19:10–22.
46. Rooker, *Leviticus*, 274. If a priest marries someone who has been sexually active before the marriage, the male son's legitimacy for priesthood is called into question.
47. Wenham, *Leviticus*, 292.

The broader family of the priests is also impacted by their position of holiness. If the daughter of a priest profanes herself by becoming a prostitute, she is to be put to death (Lev. 21:9). If a priest were to allow a prostitute to live under his roof, he would be disqualified to render decisions for the community.[48] Priests with physical defects were unqualified for priestly service (vv. 17–21),[49] but they could partake of the benefits of the offerings that were brought (v. 22). But priests in a state of uncleanness could not partake of the offerings until they were restored (22:1–9). Finally, only those within the priest's family could eat from the offerings presented on the altar (vv. 10–16). These regulations show that there were clear distinctions between the people and the priests because the priests had a greater status of holiness.

The Nazirite Vow

An ordinary Israelite could attain a greater level of holiness like that of the priests[50] by taking the vow of a Nazirite to sepa-rate himself or herself to the Lord. The vow consisted of not eating or drinking anything produced by the grapevine, not cutting the hair during the period of the vow,[51] and not touching a dead body—even for the sake of a close family member (Num. 6:1–8). These regulations clearly set the Nazirites apart from other Israelites. They were not to participate in normal activities

48. Rooker, *Leviticus*, 275.
49. Currid, *Leviticus*, 282. A priest who is physically flawless represents holiness.
50. The parallels between the priests and the Nazirites are seen in the general prohibitions against wine and against polluting oneself by contact with a dead body. Neither the Nazirite nor the high priest can touch a dead body. The Nazirite vow is more stringent in relationship to wine; the Nazirite is forbidden wine at all times, but the priests are forbidden only when they are serving in the Tent of Meeting (Ashley, *Numbers*, 141). Women could not serve as priests, but they could take a Nazirite vow to attain this special status of holiness.
51. Ibid., 143. Neither the priests nor other Israelites had this special mark of con-secration. Both the high priest's diadem (Ex. 29:6) and the Nazirite's hair (Num. 6:9, 18) are called *nezer*.

of life because they were consecrated to the Lord alone.[52] At the end of the period of the vow, the appropriate sacrifices had to be offered, the hair had to be shaved and presented to the Lord, and a wave offering had to be presented. These actions brought an end to the period of the vow.

The Ministry of the High Priest

The high priest was set apart from the other priests by the garments he wore (Ex. 28) and the actions he performed on the Day of Atonement (Lev. 16). He would go into the Most Holy Place once a year to present the blood of the sacrifices to make atonement. No one else was in the tabernacle when the high priest went into the Most Holy Place, because only one person could act as mediator.[53] He had to take precautions so that he would not die, because the Most Holy Place was the place of God's presence. God appeared in the cloud above the mercy seat (v. 2). When the high priest went inside, he was to put incense on the fire so that the cloud of incense would cover the mercy seat and keep him from viewing the presence of God (vv. 12–13). He also did not wear his normal high priestly garments; after he had bathed his body with water (v. 4), he put on linen garments with a linen turban. These garments signified the humility of the priest in seeking forgiveness for the people.[54] He also needed to offer a bull as a sin offering for his own sins and the sins of his house (v. 6). The blood was taken into the Most Holy Place and was sprinkled in front of the mercy seat. Two goats were brought forward. One goat became a sin offering for the people, and the other became the scapegoat.[55] The blood of the sacrificed

---

52. A person would take this vow out of devotion to God or to be closer to him (Longman, *Immanuel*, 148–49).

53. Rooker, *Leviticus*, 219.

54. Currid, *Leviticus*, 215.

55. Debate surrounds the meaning of the Hebrew word *azazel* (עֲזָאזֵל). The rendering *scapegoat* is taken from the verb עָזַל (*azal*), which means "go away" (supported by

goat was taken into the Most Holy Place and sprinkled before the mercy seat to make atonement for the Holy Place because of the people's transgressions. Blood from the bull and the goat were then sprinkled on the altar of burnt offering (vv. 18–19) to consecrate it for another year of service to the Lord. The shedding of blood was necessary to make atonement for the high priest, for the people, and for the tabernacle.

The live goat was then presented (Lev. 16:20–22). The high priest laid both his hands on the head of the goat and confessed over it the sin of the people of Israel. This was a comprehensive confession, for the word *all* was used with three words for *sin*: *iniquity, transgression,* and *sin.* The live goat was then sent out into the wilderness to bear the sin of the people.[56] The sins of the Israelites were completely removed. This goat pictured the removal of guilt, which was a result of the atonement.[57] An important aspect of this ritual was the ministry of the high priest in confessing sin on behalf of the people.

The role of the priests in the Old Testament was very important, but it was limited because they served at a sanctuary that was only an earthly copy of the heavenly reality, a mere shadow of things to come. The reality toward which the sacrifices pointed came in Jesus Christ. The role of the priests and the sacrificial system is fulfilled in a much greater way in the work of Christ.

Study Questions

1. Discuss the various ways in which the priests were set apart to accomplish their ministry.

---

the Septuagint and the Vulgate). Other options for *azazel* include the meaning "entire removal," a reference to the place where the goat departed or to a demon in the wilderness (Rooker, *Leviticus*, 216–17).

56. The verb that means "to bear" (*nasa*, נשא) is also used in Isaiah 53:4, 12.
57. Rooker, *Leviticus*, 221.

2. What is the origin of the role of the Levites in assisting the priests in their work?
3. What functions are given to the Levites in Numbers 2–4? Why was this work important?
4. Why was it necessary for the priests to be obedient in carrying out their work in the tabernacle?
5. What did the teaching of the priests emphasize? What was the impact of their teaching?
6. What was the purpose of the priests' blessing the people?
7. Why would an Israelite take the Nazirite vow?
8. What important work did the high priest do every year?

5

CHRIST AS PRIEST: CONSECRATED AS MEDIATOR FOR GOD'S PEOPLE

DURING JESUS' EARTHLY ministry the terms *Prophet* and *King* are used to describe Jesus. People thought that he might be the Prophet based on his teaching and his miracles. Chapter 3 has shown that Jesus is the Prophet about whom the Old Testament spoke. People were also looking for a Davidic King to come and deliver the Jewish people from the Roman government. Chapter 7 will show that Jesus is the Davidic King who has come to establish a kingdom. It is significant that the term *Priest* is not used during Jesus' earthly ministry.[1] His ministry after his ascension into heaven is described by the book of Hebrews as a priestly ministry; in fact, he is our Great High Priest (Heb. 4:14–16). There are several reasons why Jesus is not identified as a Priest during his earthly life but is identified as our High Priest after his ascension. First, Jesus is not from the tribe of

---

1. Eugene Merrill comments, "The Gospels are virtually silent with respect to any priestly aspect of Jesus' messianic office, and Paul likewise gave scant attention to Jesus as priest." "Royal Priesthood: An Old Testament Messianic Motif," *BSac* 150 (January–March 1993): 51.

Levi but from the tribe of Judah. This lineage would have kept him from ministering as a priest in the temple at Jerusalem. Second, his priestly lineage is of a higher order than the earthly lineage of the Levitical priests because he will serve as Priest in the heavenly temple. Third, Jesus does not just fulfill the Old Testament offices of prophet and priest; rather, he transforms them.[2] He is not just another prophet proclaiming the word given him from God; he is the Word itself, with the power to transform people. He is not just another priest from the lineage of Levi; he has a heavenly lineage that will equip him for serving in the heavenly tabernacle. Jesus' deity transforms these offices as he fulfills them.

The Earthly Ministry of Jesus and the Old Testament Priesthood

Consecrated to God's Service

Just because Jesus is not called a Priest during his earthly ministry does not mean that he never reflects the work of the Old Testament priests. It is beneficial to think about the earthly ministry of Jesus in light of the work of the priests. The Old Testament priests were set apart as holy to the Lord in a number of ways (see chapter 4). They were set apart by their hereditary, priestly lineage through Aaron. The priestly lineage of Jesus does not come through Aaron, but he is still set apart in his priesthood "according to the order of Melchizedek" (see below) and in his special birth. The Gospels make it clear that Mary is pregnant by the power of the Holy Spirit even though she is a virgin (Matt. 1:18–25; Luke 1:26–38). The virgin birth safeguards both the deity

2. George W. Stroup III, "The Relevance of the *Minus Triplex* for Reformed Theology and Ministry," *Austin Seminary Bulletin* 98 (1983): 29.

and the humanity of Christ.[3] His supernatural birth indicates that he is God, that his origin is heaven (John 3:13), and that he was with the Father from eternity (1:1; 8:58; 17:5). This birth is necessary for the salvation that Jesus came to accomplish. If he had been born by ordinary generation, he would have inherited Adam's guilt and would have been unable to save others.[4] His birth also demonstrates his humanity, for God takes to himself human nature by becoming the son of a woman. This is important for his work as Priest, for as a human being he is able to sympathize with people in their suffering (Heb. 4:15).

The Anointed One

The lives of the Old Testament priests were consecrated for service to the Lord by the garments they wore, by the blood of the sacrifice being applied—to their right earlobes, right thumbs, and right big toes—and by being anointed with oil. The role of the Holy Spirit in the birth and the earthly ministry of Jesus also consecrated him for service. Anointing with oil became associated with the Holy Spirit in the Old Testament (Isa. 61:1; Zech. 4:1–14). The oil meant that the individual was set apart for service, and the Holy Spirit enabled that service to be carried out. The Holy Spirit caused the Child conceived in Mary to be holy (Luke 1:35).[5] The activity of the Holy Spirit with respect to Christ's human nature continued throughout his life until his exaltation. Jesus is set apart through his supernatural birth, and it becomes clear early in his life that there is something distinctive about him. Luke comments that "the child grew and became

3. John M. Frame, *Systematic Theology: An Introduction to Christian Belief* (Phillipsburg, NJ: P&R Publishing, 2013), 886–87.

4. William Hendriksen, *Exposition of the Gospel according to Matthew* (Grand Rapids: Baker, 1973), 143.

5. Louis Berkhof, *Systematic Theology* (Grand Rapids: Eerdmans, 1941), 335. He states that the Holy Spirit "sanctified the human nature of Christ in its very inception, and thus kept it free from the pollution of sin."

strong, filled with wisdom. And the favor of God was upon him" (2:40). This wisdom is demonstrated when he is twelve years old and is found at the temple sitting among the teachers, listening to them, and asking them questions. All who heard him were amazed at his understanding and his answers (vv. 46–47). Jesus told his parents, who had been looking for him, that he must be about his Father's business. The Spirit descended on Jesus at his baptism (Matt. 3:16), filled him completely (Luke 4:1, 18), and led him into the wilderness and then to Galilee (Matt. 4:1; Luke 4:14). The Holy Spirit gave him power to cast out demons (Matt. 12:28) and to offer himself up to God without blemish (Heb. 9:14). He was declared the Son of God by his resurrection from the dead (Rom. 1:4), was made alive, ascended into heaven (1 Peter 3:18–22), and manifests himself as the life-giving Spirit (1 Cor. 15:45; 2 Cor. 3:17–18). He is filled with the Spirit without measure (John 3:34).[6] His whole life is empowered by the Spirit and lived in the fullness of the Spirit.

Jesus identified himself as the Anointed One who fulfills Isaiah 61:1 (Luke 4:16–21). He is recognized as the Messiah by Andrew, the brother of Simon Peter (John 1:41). The term *Messiah* is from the verb *to anoint*, and it means "Christ."[7] Jesus is the Messiah, the One anointed by God through the power of the Holy Spirit to carry out his ministry. Jesus' whole life is dedicated to the service of his Father in heaven. Just as the blood was placed on the right earlobe of the priests in the Old Testament, Jesus listens to his Father in heaven to faithfully carry out his Father's will. Jesus made known the name of his Father to the

6. Herman Bavinck, *Reformed Dogmatics*, vol. 3, *Sin and Salvation in Christ* (Grand Rapids: Baker, 2006), 292–93.

7. The Hebrew verb that means "to anoint" is *mashakh*, from which the noun *mashiakh* comes. In the NT, the Greek verb is *chriō* and the noun is *Christos*. Holders of the three offices of prophet, priest, and king are all anointed with oil in the OT (see chapter 1), but the kingly role became particularly associated with the coming Anointed One. D. A. Carson, *The Gospel according to John* (Grand Rapids: Eerdmans, 1991), 156. What the term *Messiah* truly means for Jesus is explained in the Gospels.

disciples, and he gave them the words that the Father had given him (17:6–8). He submitted to the truth of the Word of God and consecrated his life to the service of God so that the disciples would be sanctified in the truth (vv. 17–18).

Just as the right thumbs of the priests were set apart by the blood to signify that they were ready to do the work of God, so Jesus does the work that his Father gave him to do. John the Baptist had questions about "the deeds of the Christ," so he sent his disciples to ask Jesus whether he was the One who is to come (Matt. 11:1–3). Jesus responds by pointing to the work he is doing in line with Isaiah 61:1–4. In response to opposition he faced from a healing he performed on the Sabbath, he answered, "My Father is working until now, and I am working" (John 5:17). The working of God the Father and the working of Jesus the Son are closely aligned. On the one hand, Jesus does nothing on his own but only what he sees the Father doing, because he does the work that the Father has given him to do (vv. 19–20). On the other hand, Jesus' power and works are on the same level as the Father's. He has life in himself, as the Father has life in himself (v. 26), and he is able to grant the power of life both spiritually (vv. 24–25) and physically (vv. 28–29).[8]

Just as the right big toes of the priests were set apart by blood, signifying that they were ready to do the will of God, Jesus also goes where he is led to accomplish his mission. He was led by the Spirit into the wilderness to be tempted (Luke 4:1), and he returned in the power of the Spirit to begin his public ministry in Galilee (v. 14). At the proper time Jesus began his trip to Jerusalem with resolve, because he knew what awaited him there (9:51). He wrestled with his approaching death in the garden of Gethsemane, but he submitted to his Father's will and went

8. For a discussion of the relationship between the deity of Jesus and his subordination to the Father in John 5, see Robert L. Reymond, *Jesus Divine Messiah* (Ross-shire, UK: Christian Focus, 2003), 229–32.

CHRIST AS PRIEST: CONSECRATED AS MEDIATOR FOR GOD'S PEOPLE

boldly to the cross (22:39–46; John 18:6). Jesus' whole life was consecrated to do the will of his Father in heaven for the benefit of those whom the Father had given to him.

Guarding and Keeping God's People

Clearing the Temple. The various functions of the Levites can be summarized under the two verbs *to guard (shamar)* and *to serve/work (avad)*, which occur in Numbers 3:7–8.[9] Jesus fulfilled these functions in a limited way when he cleared the temple in Jerusalem (Matt. 21:12–13; Mark 11:15–19; Luke 19:45–48; John 2:13–22).[10] The temple was meant to be a house of prayer for quiet, spiritual devotion and fellowship.[11] It had turned into a noisy marketplace where animals were sold and money was exchanged. This activity was meant to help those who had traveled long distances for worship. They could buy animals for sacrifice with the money required by the temple. The merchants, however, charged exorbitant prices so that worship became a burden to the people. Jesus' description of their activity as a "den of robbers" is accurate.[12] The priests failed the people by not serving them (*avad*),[13] and they failed God by not guarding (*shamar*) the holiness of his house. Jesus acted as guardian of the holiness of the temple by seeking to restore its proper use as a house of prayer for all people. He cleared out the merchants by driving away those who bought and sold in the temple, and he overturned the tables of the moneychangers. An interesting comment in Mark reminds the reader of the role of the Levites. Mark adds

9. These two verbs were also used of Adam's work in the garden in Genesis 2:15.
10. For a discussion of John's placement of this incident early in Jesus' ministry rather than near the time of his death, as in the Synoptic Gospels, see Carson, *John*, 176–78.
11. Hendriksen, *Matthew*, 769.
12. Herman N. Ridderbos, *Matthew* (Grand Rapids: Zondervan, 1987), 385–86. The buying and selling took place in the court of the Gentiles, an area of the temple that they were allowed to enter.
13. In other words, they did not work on behalf of the people.

that Jesus "would not allow anyone to carry anything through the temple" (Mark 11:16). The Levites guarded the tabernacle, protecting it from anyone who should not be there, so that the wrath of God would not fall on the people (Num. 1:53; 3:10). Jesus cleared out what was improper and then guarded the temple so that it could function as a place of prayer.

Jesus' actions in the temple were strong and forceful. He used a whip of cords to drive out the sellers and the animals (John 2:15). He poured out the coins of the moneychangers and overturned their tables. These actions were motivated by zeal for the proper use of the Lord's house. The disciples connected these actions to Psalm 69:9, which states, "Zeal for your house has consumed me." Psalm 69 is a psalm of David, who called upon God to save him from those who hated him without cause (vv. 1–4). Those who were against David included his own brothers (v. 8). David prayed that others who hope in God would not be put to shame or dishonored because of him. The reproach and dishonor that David experienced were for the sake of God (vv. 6–7). The motivation was that zeal for God's house had consumed him (v. 9). David was passionate about the honor of God, and he was willing to suffer for the sake of God's purposes. In the same way, Jesus was passionate that the honor of God be guarded in the house of God. The sellers and moneychangers were dishonoring God because their activity in the temple took away from its real purpose. Jesus was willing to suffer reproach from his own people and his family for the sake of God's purposes.[14]

Zeal for God. Jesus also fulfilled the priestly, Levitical role by his zeal for the house of God. Malachi 3:1–3 comments that when the Lord whom they seek suddenly comes to his temple, he will purify the Levites and refine them like gold so that they will bring offerings in righteousness to the Lord. Jesus' actions

---

14. John shows that the opposition to Jesus included his brothers and the members of his own household (7:1–9).

of clearing the temple were meant to purify it so that proper worship could be offered by the people. The motivation for such actions can also be seen in a previous priest, from the tribe of Levi, who acted with zeal to protect the honor of God.

When the Israelites engaged in idolatry and sexual immorality with the people of Moab, Phinehas pierced a man and a woman through with a spear. This act turned back the wrath of God from the people of Israel. God states that Phinehas "was jealous with my jealousy . . . , so that I did not consume the people of Israel in my jealousy" (Num. 25:11). The Hebrew term *jealousy* expresses a strong emotion whereby the subject desires some quality or object. The basic meaning is "zeal," and when the zeal is for what belongs to someone else, it is "envy." When the zeal is for what rightfully belongs to a person, the meaning is "jealousy" in a positive sense. As Israel's husband, God is zealous that his people be faithful to the covenant. Idolatry is spiritual adultery. He acts to maintain their relationship, sometimes through judgment and sometimes through salvation.[15] Phinehas's zeal was the same zeal that God expressed for his people ("my jealousy"). Such zeal is what motivates strong, forceful action for the sake of God's honor.

Phinehas can be seen as a type of Christ. Although his actions and Jesus' actions are not the same, they have the same motivation. There is a pattern in the Old Testament of actions motivated by zeal for God's honor (Elijah in 1 Kings 19:10, Jehu in 2 Kings 10:16, and David in Psalm 69:9). Phinehas fits this pattern in a broad way. Not only is he motivated by the honor of God, but the results of his actions are similar to the results of Jesus' actions. In Numbers 25:11 his actions turn back the wrath of God from the people of Israel. Jesus' action of clearing the temple is a precursor of what his work on the cross will accomplish. He will

15. Leonard J. Coppes, קָנָא, *TWOT*, 2:802. The Septuagint translates this Hebrew word with the same word used in John 2 (*zelos*).

turn away the wrath of God from his people and establish a new place where his presence will dwell (see below). Psalm 106:30–31 also mentions Phinehas in a history of the rebellion of God's people. The psalm begins with a declaration of thanksgiving for the steadfast love of the Lord demonstrated in his mighty deeds (vv. 1–2). Those who observe justice and do righteousness at all times receive a blessing (v. 3). In light of the psalm's content, which focuses on the sinfulness of the people, it is impossible for God's people to do righteousness at all times. At the end of the psalm is a cry for God to gather his people from the nations.[16] The act of Phinehas stopped the plague, and it was "counted to him as righteousness from generation to generation forever" (v. 31). There are parallels between the language of Genesis 15:6 and Psalm 106:31, but it is clear in the context of Psalm 106 that this is not teaching salvation by works (the ideal of keeping righteousness at all times is impossible). Rather, Phinehas does not act as an individual Israelite but acts in his office as priest, in which his actions are done on behalf of the people. This is not a personal righteousness but a righteousness related to his priestly office, which was accepted by God as an act of righteous mediation on behalf of the people. Thus he serves as a type of Christ who fulfills righteousness at all times so that his actions can be counted as righteousness for himself and for his people.

In John's account of the clearing of the temple, the Jews asked Jesus for a sign to demonstrate his authority to act in such a way. Jesus answered, "Destroy this temple, and in three days I will raise it up" (John 2:19). Of course, the Jews thought he was talking about the literal temple, but Jesus was speaking about the temple of his body. He himself was the reality of what the

16. Psalm 106 is the final psalm of Book 4 of the Psalter. The cry to "save us" at the end of the psalm is answered in Psalm 107, the first psalm of Book 5. For more on these two psalms and the question of the organization of the Psalter, see Richard P. Belcher Jr., *The Messiah and the Psalms* (Ross-shire, UK: Christian Focus, 2006).

temple represented: the dwelling of God among his people.[17] He identified his own body with the temple and promised to raise it up in three days. The literal temple will no longer be the focus of worship, but God will seek worshipers who worship in spirit and truth (4:24).[18] This new community will be composed of followers of Jesus Christ, the people given to him by the Father (17:6). Jesus confirmed that he had fulfilled his responsibility of keeping them and guarding them (v. 12). This is an allusion to the work of Adam in the garden, part of which was to guard it. These two verbs are also used of the work of the Levites in the tabernacle.[19] Jesus fulfilled this important work by establishing the new community of God's people, the new temple (1 Cor. 3:16–17; 6:19–20), and by keeping them (1 John 5:18).

Teaching the People of God. Jesus guarded and kept his disciples in specific ways during his earthly ministry. The accounts of the clearing of the temple in Mark and Luke emphasize the teaching ministry of Jesus, especially concerning how the temple should properly function as a house of prayer (Mark 11:17). It was Jesus' practice to teach daily in the temple during his final days in Jerusalem (Luke 19:47). Although his work on the cross would lead to a new temple community, he supported the temple work by sending those cleansed from leprosy to the temple (17:11–14) and by paying the temple tax (Matt. 17:24–27). He also taught the true understanding of the law over the oral tradition that had

17. Edmund P. Clowney, "The Final Temple," *WTJ* 35, 2 (1972): 173–75. See also the extensive discussion of the temple in G. K. Beale, *The Temple and the Church's Mission: A Biblical Theology of the Dwelling Place of God* (Downers Grove, IL: InterVarsity Press, 2004).

18. Although Jesus supported the temple, his ministry laid the groundwork for a new spiritual temple. He circumvented the temple by directly forgiving sins (Matt. 12), and he placed himself at the center of the feasts (John 7–8). See Michael Horton, *The Christian Faith* (Grand Rapids: Zondervan, 2011), 488. For how Jesus fulfills the feasts, see John R. Sittema, *Meeting Jesus at the Feast: Israel's Festivals and the Gospel* (Grandville, MI: Reformation Fellowship, 2010).

19. The verb *guard* (*phulassō*) is used by the Septuagint to translate the Hebrew word *keep* (*shamar*) in Genesis 2:15 and Numbers 3:7.

grown up around it (5:17–48). He taught the truth of God's Word and turned many away from iniquity (Mal. 2:6). His teaching ministry continues after his ascension through the Holy Spirit, who guides the apostles to the truth (John 14:26; 15:26; 16:13).

Praying for God's People. Another way that Jesus guarded and kept his disciples during his earthly ministry was by praying for them. The regular times of prayer in Jesus' life (see chapter 3) must have included praying for his disciples. One such prayer is recorded in Luke 22:31, where Jesus tells Peter that Satan has demanded to have Peter, that he might sift him like wheat. The goal of Satan is to destroy Peter's faith, because Jesus' specific prayer for Peter is that his faith would not fail. It is likely that Peter is not the only apostle for whom Jesus prayed in light of the plural *you* in verse 31.[20] Jesus also prays for the ones given to him by the Father (John 17:9). He keeps them and guards them through prayer so that not one of them is lost, except the son of destruction (v. 12). The perseverance of the disciples' faith was based on the intercession of the earthly Jesus.[21] The fact that Judas, the betrayer, fell away was not only "that the Scripture might be fulfilled" (v. 12), but also because Satan entered into Judas (Luke 22:3). If the apostles were kept by Jesus' prayers for them, this implies that Jesus did not pray such a prayer for Judas.[22] The point is that Jesus' ministry of intercession for his people began before his ascension. In fact, Jesus even prayed for future believers in John 17:20. Although his ascension and exaltation would be very important for his continuing priestly role (see below), Jesus' intercession was not rooted in his status as ascended Lord, but in his role as Son to the Father (Luke 10:21–22).[23]

20. David Crump, *Jesus the Intercessor: Prayer and Christology in Luke–Acts* (Grand Rapids: Baker, 1992), 157, 159–61.
21. Ibid., 157.
22. Ibid., 162. This may parallel Jeremiah's not praying for the people as judgment became inevitable.
23. Ibid., 74–75.

Jesus Is Superior to the Old Testament Priests

The emphasis in this chapter has been on how Jesus fulfilled the priestly role in relationship to the garments, the anointing oil, and the work of the priests and Levites. It is clear, however, that Jesus is not from the tribe of Levi but from the tribe of Judah. This lineage disqualified him from serving as a Priest in the earthly tabernacle at Jerusalem. Jesus never officiated at the sacrifices in the tabernacle, never handled the blood of the sacrifices, and never went into the Most Holy Place as the High Priest. Jesus' lineage raises the question whether he is qualified to be a Priest for his people. The book of Hebrews answers this question with support from Old Testament Scriptures. It sets forth the superiority of Christ over the angels, Moses, and Joshua (Heb. 1:1–4:13). We are exhorted to strive to enter the rest that is still available and to not miss that rest because of disobedience (4:11). The encouragement to hold fast our confession is possible because we have a Great High Priest, Jesus the Son of God. His superiority over the earthly priests is demonstrated in his sinless humanity and in his deity (4:14–5:10). Jesus is a human being like the other priests. In the days of his flesh he suffered various trials and prayed with loud cries and tears to the One who could save him from death. He learned obedience through what he suffered (5:7–8). He was tempted in every way that human beings are tempted, but he did not sin. Thus he is able to sympathize with our weakness, and we have confidence that he will hear our prayers as we draw near to God's throne to receive grace in the time of need (4:15–16).

Jesus is superior to the earthly priests because of his divine character (Heb. 5:1–10). After his resurrection and ascension, he passed through the heavens. His ministry is not at an earthly temple but in a heavenly sanctuary.[24] Jesus, like the high priests

24. Philip E. Hughes, *A Commentary on the Epistle to the Hebrews* (Grand Rapids: Eerdmans, 1977), 170–71.

of the Old Testament, had to be appointed for this work. No priest took the honor to himself but, like Aaron, was called by God. Christ also did not exalt himself to High Priest but was appointed by God (vv. 1, 5). Two Old Testament passages support this appointment. Psalm 2:7 shows that Jesus is the Son of God, and Psalm 110:4 shows that Jesus was appointed a Priest forever according to the order of Melchizedek. Jesus fulfills the priestly role as Son, both in his humiliation and in his exaltation. Through his obedience he became the source of eternal salvation to all who obey him, being designated by God a Priest according to the order of Melchizedek (Heb. 5:8–10). There is but one Messiah, unique in his sonship and his priesthood.[25]

A Priest "according to the Order of Melchizedek"

The author of Hebrews identifies the Old Testament figure of Melchizedek from the account in Genesis 14:18–20. After Abraham defeated a confederation of kings and rescued Lot, he was met by Melchizedek, king of Salem and priest of the Most High God. Melchizedek blessed Abraham, and Abraham gave to him a tenth of the spoils of victory. Melchizedek is a mysterious figure; not much is known about him. He met Abraham in Genesis 14 and then disappeared. Melchizedek and Abraham worshiped the same God; both use the name "God Most High" (vv. 19–20, 22).[26] Melchizedek is presented as a type of Christ.[27] He is not identified with the Son of God, but he "resembles" the Son of God (Heb. 7:3). The name *Melchizedek* means "king of righteousness," and he was also king of peace based on the

25. Ibid., 181. Hughes points out that Qumran looked for two messianic figures, a royal, Davidic messiah and a priestly, Aaronic messiah. These two are fulfilled in Jesus.
26. Ibid., 246.
27. James A. Borland, *Christ in the Old Testament: Old Testament Appearances of Christ in Human Form* (Ross-shire, UK: Christian Focus, 1999), 139–47. He gives reasons why Melchizedek is not a Christophany (a preincarnate appearance of the Son of God).

name of the city of Salem over which he ruled (7:1–2). As king of righteousness and king of peace, he was a type of Christ, the messianic Priest–King. The genealogy of Melchizedek is not recorded, which is a significant omission in a book in which genealogical information is given for prominent people.[28] He is described as "without father or mother or genealogy, having neither beginning of days nor end of life" (v. 3). This describes his appearance in Genesis and is not a literal description of his life. It also sets him apart as a type of the Son of God, who is eternal.[29]

It is clear that Melchizedek was superior to Abraham and is thus superior to Abraham's descendants from the tribe of Levi (Heb. 7:4–10). This section of Hebrews begins with an exclamation of how great Melchizedek was compared to Abraham (v. 4). Hardly anyone is greater to the Jewish people than Abraham; he was the father of the nation, the one to whom God gave the covenant promises concerning his posterity.[30] The greatness of Melchizedek over Abraham is shown in two ways. First, Melchizedek blessed Abraham (Gen. 14:19–20). The inferior party is blessed by the superior party (Heb. 7:7); that makes Melchizedek the superior party. Second, Abraham paid a tithe from the spoils of victory to Melchizedek. The person who receives tithes is superior to the person who pays them. According to the law, the Levites took tithes from the people who were also descendants of Abraham. The Levites were mortal men, but the one who received the tithe from Abraham lives (vv. 5–8). We find no account of Melchizedek's death because he symbolizes a priesthood that abides eternally. This demonstrates that the priesthood of Melchizedek is greater than the Levitical priesthood, which is composed of men who

28. William Hendriksen and Simon J. Kistemaker, *Thessalonians, the Pastorals, and Hebrews* (Grand Rapids: Baker, 1995), 185.

29. Hughes, *Hebrews*, 248.

30. Ibid., 251. Hughes highlights that Abraham is called "the patriarch" (Heb. 7:4), the ancestral founder of the Hebrew people.

die. The author further argues that Levi himself paid tithes to Melchizedek through Abraham, since Levi was in his loins when Melchizedek met him (vv. 9–10). Melchizedek was greater than Abraham, and the priesthood according to Melchizedek was greater than the Levitical priesthood.

The author of Hebrews is laying a foundation to argue for the necessity of a change in the priesthood. He continues that argument by showing the deficiencies in the Levitical priesthood (7:11–22). A change of priesthood was needed because perfection had not been attained under the Levitical priests; otherwise, there would not be a need for another priest after the order of Melchizedek. The Levitical priesthood is also associated with the giving of the law (v. 11). The law and priesthood belonged together, so a change in the priesthood necessitates a change in the law. In verse 13 the author begins to show what this means for Christ as Priest. He is descended from the tribe of Judah, which has no connection to the priesthood. No one from Judah has ever served at the altar, and nothing is said about priests' coming from this tribe. The need for a change in priesthood becomes more evident when one sees the basis for Christ serving as Priest. Christ serves not on the basis of a legal requirement concerning bodily descent but by the power of his indestructible life (v. 16). The character of Christ as divine necessitates an order of priesthood that fits his divinity. Here Psalm 110:4b is quoted: "You are a priest forever after the order of Melchizedek." Christ is not susceptible to death, so he serves as a Priest forever and introduces a better hope by which to draw near to God (Heb. 7:19). With the coming of Christ, the priestly order was transformed: he fulfilled the law and made the Levitical priesthood obsolete.[31]

31. Simon J. Kistemaker, *Exposition of the Epistle to the Hebrews* (Grand Rapids: Baker, 1984), 192. The fact that the Levitical priesthood is obsolete would seem to go against Jeremiah 33:18, "and the Levitical priests shall never lack a man in my presence to offer burnt offerings," which parallels God's promise that David will never lack a man on

The Benefits of Christ's Priesthood

Part of the argument for a change of priesthood is the benefits to God's people that it would accomplish. Several benefits are covered in the book of Hebrews. The superior nature of the priesthood according to the order of Melchizedek is demonstrated by its establishment by oath (Ps. 110:4a). The priesthood of Aaron and his sons was enacted by a statute (Ex. 29:9) but not by an oath. The oath sets the appointment of Christ as Priest apart from the Levitical priests and makes him the guarantor of a better covenant (Heb. 7:22). The priesthood (v. 11) and the Mosaic covenant (Jer. 31:32) could not bring about perfection. The superior priesthood lasts forever based on the character of Jesus and cannot be annulled or set aside because he is the guarantor of the covenant. The service of Christ as Priest is better than the service of the Old Testament priests because he is a permanent Priest not impacted by death. This implies that he is always able to make intercession for his people and that he is able to save them completely (Heb. 7:23–25). The character of Jesus sets him apart from the Levitical priests and affects his priestly ministry. He is holy, innocent, unstained, separated from sinners, and exalted above the heavens. He is the Son who has been made perfect forever. Thus he does not need to offer daily sacrifices for his own sins. He also does not need to offer daily sacrifices for the people's sins because his sacrifice on the cross for salvation was sufficient once for all (7:26–28; 10:11–14). The ministry of Jesus as Priest is not carried out in the

---

the throne (Jer. 33:17). Christ fulfills the OT offices and transforms them so that they continue in greater ways. He sits on the throne of David; this is not an earthly throne but the heavenly throne at the right hand of the Father. Christ transforms the temple and the priesthood so that the ministry of the church, the new temple of God, is carried out by the sacrifices of his people. This fulfills Isaiah 66:21 in that Gentiles are able to serve as priests and Levites. Clowney ("Final Temple," 170) points out that even if an earthly temple were rebuilt in Jerusalem, Christ the risen Lord would be barred from that sanctuary while the sons of Levi would mediate between him and the Father. There is no need for an earthly temple, just as there is no need for continued offering of sacrifices (Heb. 10:11–18).

earthly tabernacle, a copy and shadow of the heavenly, but in the heavenly sanctuary (8:4–5). This point is made several times in Hebrews 9–10. Christ entered the greater and more perfect tent once for all to offer his own blood to secure eternal redemption (9:11–14). He does not have to enter the Most Holy Place every year to offer himself repeatedly; he appeared once for all to put away sin by his sacrifice (9:23–28; 10:11–14).

Christ could never have accomplished this work of complete salvation if he had been a priest in the line of Aaron serving in the earthly tabernacle. The blood of bulls and goats could not permanently take away sin (Heb. 10:4). For eternal redemption to be secured, Christ had to be a Priest according to the order of Melchizedek. His divine character and indestructible life meant that the onetime sacrifice of himself fulfilled the righteousness of God and paid for sin. Christ's obedience and perfection (4:15; 5:7–9) are important because the salvation of the people of God depends on the priest's being obedient to God's commands (Lev. 10:1–3). At his resurrection and ascension into heaven he entered the heavenly tent and presented his work to his Father for the salvation of his people. In contrast to the Levitical priests, who stand daily because their work is never finished, Christ sat down at the right hand of God because his work of sacrifice was finished.[32] His priestly work continues in his continual intercession for his people. As the One who bore their sin, he is able to confess their sin so that their transgressions can be forgiven (Lev. 16:21; Isa. 53:12). His ongoing intercession means that there is present, continual help for the people of God (Heb. 4:16). The work of Christ as Priest ensures that his people will not fall away but that they will come through every trial. The benefits include the forgiveness of sin, the cleansing of the conscience, peace with God, assurance of salvation, and the gift of eternal life. Believers are also perfected by being set apart to live a life of

32. Hughes, *Hebrews*, 400.

holiness, which will result in the completion of their perfection when Christ comes again (10:14).[33]

Blessing the People of God

The role of a priest included blessing the people of God. Just as Melchizedek blessed Abraham (Gen. 14:19; Heb. 7:1, 6) and the priests blessed the people (Lev. 9:22; Num. 6:22–27), so Jesus blessed his disciples at his ascension (Luke 24:50). As the resurrected Lord, he lifted up his hands and blessed his disciples as he was carried up into heaven.[34] As the ascended Lord, he continues his ministry on behalf of his people. Christ as our Advocate (1 John 2:1) pleads the believer's cause with the Father in heaven against the false accusations brought against God's people (Heb. 7:25; 1 John 2:1; Rev. 12:10), and through the Holy Spirit believers are strengthened to carry out their ministry in this world (John 16:8). Christ continues to pray for the spiritual needs of his people, for their protection, and for their perseverance in the faith so that they will participate in his victory. In Revelation, Christ is the Lamb who receives the prayers of the saints in bowls of incense and is worthy to open the scroll, because through his blood he ransomed a people for God from every tribe and nation (Rev. 5:6–10). This Lamb is the King of kings who conquers the beasts of Revelation (17:14). In the description of his coming to lead the armies of heaven into the last great battle, he is described as wearing a robe dipped in blood (19:13). The Priest who suffered for his people now comes to conquer all their enemies.

---

33. Kistemaker, *Hebrews*, 282.
34. William Hendriksen, *Exposition of the Gospel according to Luke* (Grand Rapids: Baker, 1978), 1076. He comments that this blessing is an effective impartation of welfare, peace, and power.

Study Questions

1. Why isn't Jesus identified as a Priest during his earthly ministry? Does this mean that we should not think about the work of Jesus in terms of a Priest? Why or why not?
2. How was Jesus set apart or consecrated for his work?
3. How does Jesus fulfill the role of guarding and keeping the temple and his people during his earthly ministry? In what ways do these examples expand your view of the ministry of Jesus?
4. How is Christ superior to the Old Testament priests?
5. How does Christ relate to the figures of Phinehas and Melchizedek?
6. List some benefits of Christ's priesthood. How do these benefits impact your life as a Christian?

6

THE ROLE OF THE KING IN THE OLD TESTAMENT

THE ROLE OF DOMINION given to mankind in Genesis 1 lays the foundation for kingship in redemptive history. This culminates in Jesus Christ and will have implications for the continuing role of human beings in ruling over and caring for God's creation.

The Seed of the Woman

God created mankind (*adam*, אָדָם) to exercise dominion over creation. Every human being, created in the image of God, is to rule over creation for the glory of God (Gen. 1:26–28). His rule on the earth was accomplished through human beings, carrying out their God-given role under his authority. Adam and Eve rejected his authority by disobeying his command, and their rebellion brought God's good creation under the curse and power of sin (3:14–19). They failed to exercise dominion over the serpent by not casting him out of the garden. In turn, they were cast out of the garden. Someone from the seed of the woman will have to come to defeat the serpent, to rescue creation from the curse of sin, and to restore the proper role of dominion to human beings (v. 15).

Because of sin, mankind no longer lives in harmony with creation, so the exercise of dominion becomes hard work. The presence of sin not only impacts humans' relationship to creation, but also distorts both the vertical relationship between humanity and God and the horizontal relationships between human beings. Dominion can easily become domination, exploitation, and oppression. These characteristics are exemplified in Genesis 4 with the triumph and escalation of sin. Cain murders his brother Abel. Lamech takes two wives (contrary to 2:24) and boasts of killing a young man. The widespread nature of sin is stated in Genesis 6:5: "The LORD saw that the wickedness of man was great in the earth, and that every intention of the thoughts of his heart was only evil continually." God responds to the pervasive sin on the earth with the judgment of the flood (6:9–8:19). Noah emerges after the flood as a new Adam with the continuing responsibility of dominion in a fallen world.[1] The animals will fear human beings, and justice needs to be established by protecting human life (9:2–6). God's covenant with Noah ensures that God will no longer destroy the earth with a flood, and that the cycles of creation (seedtime and harvest, summer and winter, day and night) will continue to allow human beings to carry out his mandate to multiply and fill the earth (8:20–9:17).

A Son of Abraham

The drunkenness of Noah (Gen. 9:20–27) and the Tower of Babel incident (11:1–9) show the continuing problem of sin. Noah abuses the good gift of wine, and the people of Babel desire to make a name for themselves. God begins to work through Abram

---

1. Victor P. Hamilton, *The Book of Genesis: Chapters 1–17* (Grand Rapids: Eerdmans, 1990), 313.

and his family to restore the dominion that was lost at the fall. Abram, like Adam and Noah, has the opportunity to carry out God's original purpose for human beings.[2] Abram exercises a kingly role by rescuing Lot from a coalition of kings that had conquered Sodom. God makes the covenant of circumcision with Abram, promises that Abram will be the father of a multitude of nations, and changes his name to Abraham (17:4-5).[3] God also promises Abraham that kings will come forth from him[4] and that his descendants will take possession of the land of Canaan (vv. 6-8). Thus Abraham's descendants will have the opportunity to establish God's rule by exercising dominion.

A Ruler from Judah

As redemptive history moves forward, more information is given concerning the One who will come to rule. In Genesis 3:15, the One coming to battle the serpent is from the seed of the woman. The focus narrows when God calls Abraham and makes promises about his future descendants. God develops the chosen line through Isaac, with the twelve sons of Jacob becoming the nucleus of the nation of Israel. Near the end of his life, Jacob blesses his sons and speaks concerning their future (ch. 49). A ruler will come from the tribe of Judah (vv. 8-12), who is praised by his brothers and given a place of prominence among them. They bow down before him because of his victory over his

2. Gordon J. Wenham, *Genesis 16-50* (Dallas: Word Books, 1994), 22.

3. Many nations come from Abraham, including the descendants of Ishmael (Gen. 17:16; 25:12-18) and the descendants of Esau—also called the Edomites (36:1-43)—including the Temanites, the Horites, and the Amalekites. This promise is also fulfilled through Christ (Gal. 3:29), when many nations will become part of Abraham's offspring through faith. John D. Currid, *A Study Commentary on Genesis*, vol. 1, *Genesis 1:1-25:18* (Darlington, UK: Evangelical Press, 2003), 312.

4. The promise of kings includes the tribal rulers of Ishmael (Gen. 17:16; 25:12-18), the kings of Edom (36:9-43), and the Israelite kings from the tribe of Judah (49:8-12). The ultimate fulfillment will be Jesus, the son of David, who will "reign over the house of Jacob forever, and of his kingdom there will be no end" (Luke 1:33).

enemies (v. 8). Judah is likened to a lion that conquers his prey. The lion imagery fits well with the kingly language that is used to describe his future. This victory will come through a ruler who will arise from Judah and command the obedience of the peoples.[5] The coming of this ruler will bring abundant blessing (vv. 11–12). There will be so many vines that people will not worry about hitching a donkey to one, even though this would destroy the vine. Wine will be as plentiful as water. This abundance will lead to a healthy appearance among the people (v. 12).

A Star out of Jacob

Balak, king of Moab, is concerned about the people of Israel as they travel to the land of Canaan. He is afraid that they are too numerous and powerful for him to defeat and that they will take over his land. He calls for Balaam, a diviner, to curse them (Num. 22:5–6). Balaam delivers four oracles (22:41–23:10; 23:13–26; 23:27–24:14; 24:15–19), but God will not allow him to curse Israel. In the fourth oracle (24:15–19), Balaam looks to the future and sees a ruler, called a scepter, who will come from Israel. The term *scepter* is also used in Genesis 49:10 and is a symbol of kingship. The coming One is described as a star that will come out of Jacob (Num. 24:17). The word *star* is not often used for a royal figure in the Old Testament (Isa. 14:12), but it is a common designation in the ancient Near East.[6] This ruler will defeat Moab, the sons of Sheth,[7] and Edom. This seems to be a reference to David or the Davidic dynasty because these nations are the local enemies of Israel and Judah. It is debatable whether this passage is completely fulfilled in David or whether it is messianic. David

---

5. For a discussion of the meaning of *shiloh*, see Richard P. Belcher Jr., *Genesis: The Beginning of God's Plan of Salvation* (Ross-shire, UK: Christian Focus, 2012), 268–69.

6. Timothy R. Ashley, *The Book of Numbers* (Grand Rapids: Eerdmans, 1993), 500.

7. The sons of Sheth are not the whole human race (Sethites of Adamic lineage) but are a people group from the lineage of Seth based on the parallel with Moab. R. Dennis Cole, *Numbers* (Nashville: Broadman & Holman, 2000), 427.

subdues Moab and Edom, but not permanently; Jeremiah 48–49 prophesies against Moab and Edom. The star out of Jacob refers to David but gives a glimpse of the messianic hope, even if in an indirect form, when placed in the context of the whole Bible.[8]

The Role of the King in Israel (Deuteronomy 17:14–20)

God had promised that kings would come from Abraham. Several texts have spoken of a King who would emerge from Israel and defeat her enemies (Gen. 49:8–12; Num. 24:15–19). As the people prepare to enter the land of Canaan, Moses prepares them with three addresses in Deuteronomy. He instructs them by reviewing their history (1:1–4:43), by focusing on their future life in the land (4:44–28:68), and by stressing that faithfulness to the covenant will give them a future (29:1–30:20).[9] These addresses are followed by an epilogue of the last acts of Moses, including the commissioning of Joshua.[10] The passage defining the king's role occurs in the second address in the context of setting forth the leaders of God's people. Moses speaks about judges (16:18–20),

8. Ashley, *Numbers*, 503.

9. These addresses are divided by "these are the words" (1:1), "this is the law" (4:44), and "these are the words" (29:1).

10. The book of Deuteronomy can be approached in numerous ways. It is a covenant-renewal document that parallels the covenants of the ANE. Meredith Kline, *Treaty of the Great King* (Grand Rapids: Eerdmans, 1963). For a general discussion of this relationship, see Eugene Merrill, *Deuteronomy* (Nashville: Broadman & Holman), 28–32. Some also view Deuteronomy as an exposition of the Ten Commandments. John D. Currid, *A Study Commentary on Deuteronomy* (Darlington, UK: Evangelical Press, 2006), 19–24. These views are not necessarily mutually exclusive. Others argue that Deuteronomy is the first book in the Deuteronomistic History (Deuteronomy–Kings), written in the exile to justify Judah's punishment for disregarding the word of the prophets. Martin Noth, *The Deuteronomistic History* (Sheffield, UK: JSOT Press, 1981). Many works have responded to and adjusted the original work of Noth, such as F. M. Cross, *Canaanite Myth and Hebrew Epic* (Cambridge, MA: Harvard University Press, 1973). For a textual analysis of the insights of the different approaches to Deuteronomy through 2 Samuel, see Anthony Campbell and Mark A. O'Brien, *Unfolding the Deuteronomistic History: Origins, Upgrades, Present Text* (Minneapolis: Fortress Press, 2000). For an evaluation of this view, see Merrill, *Deuteronomy*, 34–37.

priests and judges who would handle difficult cases (17:8–13), kings (17:14–20), and prophets (18:15–22).

Kings in the Ancient Near East

The main characteristic of the role of the king within Israel is the limits placed on him. He is not the highest authority in the land. This role of the king was different from the way kings functioned in other nations in the ancient Near East. In Egypt the king was the central figure of society. He was the absolute monarch and the chief executive officer of the state. He was the source of all laws and the foundation of moral righteousness. He was the supreme high priest, who was the main link between the gods and humanity. This link guaranteed the triumph of order over chaos on the earth. This universal order, called *ma'at*, was maintained by the reign of the king. He functioned as a key component of society's proper order. He held a divine office derived from the realm of the gods. No enemy could stand against him.[11]

The role of the king was understood in a variety of ways throughout Mesopotamian history.[12] In general, he was not a god but was endowed with divine vocation as the gods' representative or administrator; thus he wielded superhuman power that put him on the same plane as the gods.[13] He was

---

11. Ronald J. Leprohon, "Royal Ideology and State Administration in Pharaonic Egypt," in *Civilizations of the Ancient Near East*, ed. Jack M. Sasson (Peabody, MA: Hendrickson, 1995), 273–74. For a discussion of the concept *ma'at*, see John D. Currid, *Ancient Egypt and the Old Testament* (Grand Rapids: Baker, 1997), 118–19.

12. W. G. Lambert, "Kingship in Ancient Mesopotamia," in *King and Messiah in Israel and the Ancient Near East*, ed. John Day (Sheffield, UK: Sheffield Academic Press, 1998), 54–71.

13. J. N. Postgate, "Royal Ideology and State Administration in Sumer and Akkad," in *Civilizations of the Ancient Near East*, ed. Jack M. Sasson (Peabody, MA: Hendrickson, 2000), 397, 399. The complexity of the relationship between the king and the gods is discussed by David Beckham, "Kingship and Divinity in Imperial Assyria," in *Text, Artifact, and Image: Revealing Ancient Israelite Religion*, ed. Gary M. Beckman and Theodore J. Lewis (Providence, RI: Brown Judaic Studies, 2006), 182–88. He argues that the office, not the king, may be considered divine.

the image of the gods and their representative, filled with their divine power and authority to rule on earth.[14] Evidence of the Canaanite view of the king comes mainly from the Ugaritic texts. This evidence is not as abundant as the evidence from Egypt and Mesopotamia. The king was considered the son of the god El. Theological language sets him apart from common humanity, the priesthood, and nobility. He bridged the boundary between the divine and human orders and thus somehow shared in the divine realm.[15] As the god's viceroy, the king administered the deity's territory. One of his major roles was to ensure that justice and righteousness prevailed in the nation.[16]

Kings in the ancient Near East were the highest authority in the land. This view made it difficult for anyone to criticize their policies or actions. The role of the king in Israel was different because he was not considered to be a god or divine, and there was a higher authority over him. His power was limited in a number of ways. The recognition that Yahweh is the King of Israel limited the earthly king's authority. Yahweh fought and defeated Pharaoh and the gods of Egypt to deliver his people from bondage. The victory song after crossing the Red Sea celebrates Yahweh as a man of war (Ex. 15:3) who defeated the army of Pharaoh (vv. 4–10). Such actions will bring dread upon the inhabitants of Canaan. God will plant his people in the land, and he will reign over them (vv. 14–18). The Lord is King because of the glory of his majesty and his power to defeat all his enemies.[17]

14. Bruce K. Waltke, *Genesis* (Grand Rapids: Zondervan, 2001), 66.

15. Nicolas Wyatt, "The Religious Role of the King in Ugarit," in *Ugarit at Seventy-Five*, ed. K. Lawson Younger Jr. (Winona Lake, IN: Eisenbrauns, 2007), 41–74.

16. Gosta W. Ahlstrom, "Administration of the State in Canaan and Ancient Israel," in *Civilizations of the Ancient Near East*, 590, 598.

17. John N. Oswalt, "Exodus," in *Cornerstone Biblical Commentary*, ed. Philip W. Comfort (Carol Stream, IL: Tyndale House, 2008), 1:399. Numbers 23:21 also recognizes the Lord as the King of Israel.

Kings in Israel Rule under God's Authority

Yahweh brought the people to Mount Sinai and entered into a covenant with them. He gave them his law and took his place among them in the center of the camp (Num. 2), the place where the king would normally place his tent.[18] God led them forth toward the land of Canaan (10:35–36) and sent his heavenly commander to lead them into battle (Josh. 5:13–15).[19] Based on the way that the Israelites conquered Jericho (ch. 6) and the way that creation assisted in their victory against the five Amorite kings (10:12–14), it is clear that Yahweh fought for his people and defeated all their enemies. It did not matter if the enemies of Israel were more numerous or had more powerful weapons because no human army can defeat Yahweh (Judg. 4–5; 7). When the people came to make Gideon king, he rejected their offer with the proper response: "I will not rule over you, and my son will not rule over you; the Lord will rule over you" (8:23). Yahweh is the true King of Israel.

Statements in Deuteronomy made it clear that even if Israel appointed a human king, that king would rule under the authority of Yahweh, the true King. Yahweh established the covenant relationship, and the covenant regulated the various responsibilities of the leaders of the nation. The law of God was the standard by which the nation and her leaders, including the king, would be judged. The king was just one of the many important leaders of Israel. There was a balance of power presented in Deuteronomy 16:18–18:22 that limited the power of all offices, including the king; the laws worked together as the constitution of the nation. Thus power was not concentrated in one office, but authority

18. Tremper Longman III and Raymond B. Dillard, *An Introduction to the Old Testament*, 2nd ed. (Grand Rapids: Zondervan, 2006), 77.

19. This person identifies himself as the commander of the army of the Lord. The evidence that he is heavenly, even divine, is seen in the fact that Joshua falls on his face to worship this figure and is told to take off his sandals, for the ground on which he stands is holy (Josh. 5:15).

was found in a number of offices based on the authority of the law.[20] The king was to keep a copy of the law with him and read it all his life (17:18–20). This would keep the king humble and remind him of his true source of authority. He would learn to fear God by reading the law and keeping all its words so that his heart would not become full of pride. The king submitted to the authority of Yahweh by submitting to the law of God.[21]

At Mount Sinai Israel became a nation, but having a king to lead the nation was not a top priority. Several important leadership roles are mentioned in Deuteronomy 16–18 before the role of the king is described, such as judges (16:18–20) and priests and judges who would handle difficult cases (17:8–13). The role of the prophet is described after the king (18:15–22). The prophet will speak God's word to the king and call him and the nation back to obedience when they disobey. The way in which the role of the king is introduced shows that having a king will come with certain temptations. When the people come into the land, they will desire a king so that they can be like other nations (17:14–15). The fact that kingship is listed among the leaders of the land shows that the role itself is not wrong, but the motivation for having a king can be misguided (see the discussion on 1 Sam. 8 below). In fact, God declares that they may have a king of his choosing: "you may set a king over you, whom the LORD your God will choose" (Deut. 17:15). The point is that Israel can become a nation without a human king because Yahweh is her King.[22] Kingship will become an important role within Israel, but it will function within certain limits.

20. Patricia Dutcher-Walls, "The Circumspection of the King: Deuteronomy 17:16–17 in Its Ancient Social Context," *JBL* 121 (2002): 603–4.
21. The king is presented as a model Israelite. Duane L. Christensen, *Deuteronomy 1:1–21:9*, rev. ed. (Nashville: Thomas Nelson, 2001), 386. The picture of the king reading the law of God parallels Psalm 1, where the faithful Israelite also meditates on the law of God.
22. Peter C. Craigie, *The Book of Deuteronomy* (Grand Rapids: Eerdmans, 1976), 253. He comments that this section is the only one of its kind in the Pentateuch; it takes

Limits on the Power of the King

Certain temptations to abuse power accompany kingship. Deuteronomy 17:16–17 tried to address these temptations by limiting the actions of the king in three areas. First, the king was not to acquire many horses for himself. This restriction put a limit on the size of Israel's army. The prohibition against returning to Egypt to acquire horses may have also limited foreign alliances to secure horses for military purposes.[23] There was a great temptation to trust in the strength of the army for military victory rather than trusting in the power of Yahweh. He, however, was the One who led the people into battle, fought for them, and secured their victory. A human king was to continue to depend on the Lord for military victory.

Second, the king was not to acquire many wives for himself. This prohibition also limited foreign entanglements because many times when a treaty was made with another nation, a wife would be given to the king.[24] These wives would be foreign women who worshiped false gods, and they would bring this influence into the nation of Israel. The temptation to worship false gods would increase because of the proximity of these foreign wives to the king.

The third and final limit on the power of the king was that he should not acquire excessive silver and gold for himself. This also limited commerce with foreign nations and the king's accumulation of personal wealth, which would bring him more power and set him above other Israelites.[25] Wealth would increase his temptation to think himself above others and to disobey God (Deut. 17:20).

---

the form of permissive legislation rather than posting a requirement. It anticipates a time when kingship might become a necessity for practical and pragmatic reasons, and it specifies the characteristics required of a king in a state that was a theocracy.

23. See the discussion in ibid., 255–56.

24. Christensen, *Deuteronomy 1:1–21:9*, 388. He notes that the harem of the Middle East was a center of political intrigue and power. Solomon's many wives were an integral part of the foreign-policy system, and in direct violation of the law of the king, since each wife would represent a formal political alliance.

25. Dutcher-Walls, "The Circumspection of the King," 604.

The kings of Israel were to be different from the kings of the ancient Near East. The Israelite king did not have absolute power but shared in the administration of the law with other leaders. They were all subject to God and to his Word; in this the king was not to view himself as different from other Israelites. He would be blessed if he obeyed the law of God. He was to live in dependence on God in how he ran his court. He was not to trust in things that most kings trusted in to show their glory and power. There would be a great temptation to establish a seat of centralized power with a massive bureaucracy needing to be supported by increasing taxes. It is easy for the trappings of power to become more important than anything else. Power easily corrupts, and sadly becomes a pattern later in Israel's history.

The Need for a King: The Book of Judges

Moses fulfilled various roles within Israel, including covenant mediator, judge, prophet, and general leader of the people. He ruled over the people in his various roles, but it would be a misnomer to call him a king. The same could be said about Joshua, who took over from Moses and led Israel into the land of Canaan. His main role was as Israel's military commander to fulfill the mission that God had given to Israel: to drive out the Canaanites and to give the land to Israel as her inheritance. Joshua fulfilled that mission by breaking the Canaanites' control in the land, enabling each tribe to finish the job of driving out the Canaanites. When Joshua died, no successor was appointed to take his place. The covenant had been renewed just before Joshua's death (Josh. 24), but the Israelites had no central authority structure. God was their King, and the tribes were to complete the conquest of the land allotted to them. Although there was some initial success in driving out the Canaanites, Israel failed to complete her mission (Judg. 1). The Israelites allowed the Canaanites to remain in the land. They disobeyed God and began to worship false gods. This began a cycle: the children of Israel disobey God, he gives them into the hand of an oppressor, they cry out to the Lord, and he raises up a deliverer to save them from the oppressor (2:11–19). These deliverers—called judges—were not civil magistrates, kings with a dynasty, or officials elected by the people. They were military leaders spontaneously raised up by God to deliver the people from an oppressor.

A downward spiral in the book of Judges marks the judges themselves and the condition of the people.[26] Othniel, the first judge, is presented in an ideal way. He defeats a very powerful enemy named Cuthan-Rishathaim (the name means "dark, doubly wicked") with a simple description of victory emphasizing the role of Yahweh (Judg. 3:7–11). Ambiguity surrounds the way in which the next judge, Ehud, uses deception to kill Eglon, the king of Moab (vv. 12–30). Barak is hesitant to lead Israel into battle without being accompanied by Deborah; this leads to the statement that the glory of the victory will go to a woman (4:8–10). A significant decline occurs with Gideon because the Israelites are worse off at the end of his life than they were when he was called as judge. At the end of Gideon's life, Israel is involved in idolatry because of an ephod that Gideon made (8:22–28). The downward spiral continues when Jephthah makes a rash vow that leads to the sacrifice of his daughter (11:29–40),[27] and Samson embodies the nation of Israel when he does what is right in his own eyes (14:1–7). He disregards the Nazirite vow, he battles against the Philistines for personal revenge, and he goes after

26. Daniel I. Block speaks of the increasing intensity of the nation's depravity and develops the theme of the Canaanization of Israel during the period of the settlement. *Judges, Ruth* (Nashville: Broadman & Holman, 1999), 58.

27. Whether Jephthah actually sacrificed his daughter or whether she spent the rest of her life serving at the tabernacle is a subject of disagreement. For the latter view, see C. F. Keil and F. Delitzsch, "Judges," in *Commentary on the Old Testament*, vol. 2 (Grand Rapids: Eerdmans, 1978), 388–95. For the former view, see K. Lawson Younger Jr., *Judges and Ruth* (Grand Rapids: Zondervan, 2002), 261–67; Barry G. Webb, *The Book of Judges* (Grand Rapids: Eerdmans, 2012), 331–36.

foreign women. One of those women leads to his downfall. He ends his life, however, killing thousands of Philistines by bringing the temple down on them and himself.

Kingship is a theme in the book of Judges; more specifically, the argument is made that Israel needs a godly king to keep society from falling apart.[28] False views of kingship arise in the account of Gideon and Abimelech. The people come to Gideon and ask him to become their king. Gideon gives the right answer to their request: "I will not rule over you, and my son will not rule over you; the LORD will rule over you" (Judg. 8:23). Although Gideon rejects the offer of dynastic kingship, he later lives like a king and his son seeks to become king. Gideon names his son *Abimelech* ("my father is king"), and his death triggers a struggle for dynastic succession because Gideon had acquired a considerable harem, which produced seventy sons (v. 30). Abimelech seeks to become king through self-assertion and by eliminating Gideon's other sons. He, however, comes to a tragic end. The Canaanite—or worldly—way of becoming king does not work in Israel.

The book of Judges ends with several chapters that show the complete disintegration of Israelite society (chs. 17–21). Morality breaks down at both the national level and the individual levels. A Levite and a tribe participate in the establishment of their own religious system. A city in Benjamin acts like Sodom and Gomorrah. A Levite shows little concern for his concubine, who is abused by the inhabitants of Gibeah. The response of the other tribes of Israel against Benjamin makes matters worse. The refrain of this section is that "in those days there was no king in Israel" (18:1; 19:1), and "everyone did what was right in his own eyes" (17:6; 21:25). This refrain emphasizes that a king is needed to give spiritual

28. Block (*Judges*, 57–58) argues against the view that Judges is pro-monarchy because such a view is too political and does not emphasize other aspects of the period. And yet the political aspects of the lack of a king and the spiritual issues of apostasy are related to each other. For the view that Judges is an apologetic for the Davidic monarchy, see Keil and Delitzsch, "Judges," 247–49.

leadership to God's people. Instead of an external threat, the end of Judges describes the internal threat of the disobedience of God's people. It shows the complete breakdown of God's law, leading to sexual and social perversion. A godly king is needed to keep Israel on the path of holiness so that she can fulfill her mission.

Israel's Request for a King: The People's Choice

The deteriorating condition of society reflected in Judges continues in the book of Samuel. The word of the Lord was rare in those days (1 Sam. 3:1). The priesthood was corrupt. The sons of Eli, the priest, did not know the Lord, and they abused their position as priests for their own benefit (2:12). They stole food from the sacrifices, they slept with the women who served at the Tent of Meeting, and they did not listen to the rebuke of their father (vv. 12–25). Judgment was pronounced by a prophet against the household of Eli (vv. 27–36).

The spiritual barrenness of Israel, represented by the priests, is paralleled in the physical barrenness of Hannah. The family of Elkanah and Hannah is contrasted with the condition of the nation. Elkanah is faithful in worship, and Hannah takes her problems to God in prayer. Her physical barrenness is more than just a personal problem and becomes the avenue through which God provides for the spiritual barrenness of Israel.[29] The birth of Samuel ends Hannah's physical barrenness and is the answer to Israel's spiritual decline. Samuel becomes a godly leader who brings religious stability and fruitfulness. He is dedicated to God and grows up serving at the tabernacle in the presence of the Lord (1 Sam. 2:21). He grows in favor with the Lord and the people (v. 26), and none of his words fall to the ground because the Lord is with him (3:19).

29. John Woodhouse, *1 Samuel: Looking for a Leader* (Wheaton, IL: Crossway, 2008), 35–37.

One of Samuel's important roles is serving as a transitional figure between the era of the judges and the establishment of kingship in Israel. At the end of his life, the elders of Israel come to him to request that he appoint a king over them. His sons, who are judges, do not walk in the way of the Lord, and they turn aside after gain (1 Sam. 8:1–3). The elders ask for a king to judge them like the kings of the other nations (vv. 4–5). They also desire a king who will go before the people and fight their battles (v. 20). The divine analysis of this request is that they have rejected Yahweh as their King (v. 7). The desire to have a king is not wrong, but their motivation for a king is misguided.[30] The elders are seeking to be like the other nations instead of being a distinct nation. Israel wants a king who will give her power and political influence. Leading the nation into battle is not a right granted to the king in Deuteronomy 17. This request shows a lack of trust in Yahweh, who leads the nation and wins her battles. Yahweh fights and gives the victory not only in the book of Joshua but also in the victory over the Philistines in 1 Samuel 7. The elders now reject this arrangement in their request for a king. God tells Samuel that this request fits Israel's pattern of rebellion since the exodus from Egypt. Samuel warns the Israelites what a king will demand by showing how he will take from them (8:11–17). The people, however, are firm in their resolve to have a king (vv. 19–22).

The Lord gives them the kind of king they desire. Saul appears to have the qualifications to be king. The lengthy genealogy (1 Sam. 9:1–2) shows that he comes from a substantial family in Israel. He is an imposing figure who stands out in a crowd because he is a handsome young man and "taller than any of the people" (v. 2). He is described as a military leader (*nagid*, נגיד), and after he is publicly proclaimed king he leads the people to victory over the Ammonites (ch. 11). There are, however, negative

---

30. See Robert D. Bergen, *1, 2 Samuel* (Nashville: Broadman & Holman, 2002), 112–13.

descriptions connected to the character of Saul.[31] He is from the city of Gibeah of the tribe of Benjamin, where heinous acts of sin occurred in the book of Judges (chs. 19–20). The description of being tall is normally used for Israel's enemies (Num. 13:33; Deut. 2:10), and may indicate that Saul is like the other nations' kings. When he is publicly proclaimed king, he is found hiding among the baggage (1 Sam. 10:20–22). These negative elements are possible indications of problems with Israel's first king.

God rejects Saul as the king of Israel because he is unwilling to submit to the word of God. Before the battle with the Philistines (1 Sam. 13), Saul becomes impatient and does not wait for Samuel to arrive to offer the sacrifice. Although the people begin to scatter, Saul could have called them to faithful obedience and waited for Samuel, according to his instructions. Instead, Saul offers the sacrifice himself. Samuel confronts Saul with his disobedience, and Saul is told that his kingdom will not continue. In the battle against the Amalekites (ch. 15), Saul does not carry out the command of the Lord to devote to destruction everything captured in battle. When confronted with his sin, Saul does not repent but seeks to save face before the people. Samuel must finish the job by putting to death the king of the Amalekites. Samuel specifically states that because Saul has rejected the word of the Lord, the Lord has rejected him as king (v. 26).

David: God's Choice for King

When Saul rejected Samuel's word and offered the sacrifice before the battle with the Philistines, Samuel told Saul that his kingdom would not continue; God had sought a man after his own heart to be prince over his people Israel (1 Sam. 13:14). The phrase "a man after God's own heart" may emphasize Yahweh's

---

31. Bergen (ibid., 35–36) has a good discussion of both the positive and negative characteristics of Saul's character. He also discusses Saul beginning on page 118.

freedom to choose according to his own criteria in selecting a replacement for Saul.[32] The phrase may also speak positively about the character of the next king. He will be like-minded with the Lord and will surrender to God's word.[33]

The way in which David is chosen to be king emphasizes that he is God's choice. During a feast Samuel is sent to Jesse the Bethlehemite to anoint the next king. Samuel is impressed with the appearance of the firstborn son. The Lord's decision, however, is not based on outward appearance but on seeing the heart (1 Sam. 16:7). All the sons of Jesse pass before Samuel, but none of them is the chosen king. David, the youngest son, is tending the sheep. He was not considered significant enough to be invited to the feast, but Samuel is told that he is God's choice when he is brought in. David is anointed king in a private ceremony.

David's rise to power shows that he is a man who is willing to follow God's lead. When Goliath defies the armies of Israel and no one, including Saul, is willing to fight him, David slays him and gives Israel a great victory (1 Sam. 17). David faithfully serves Saul by playing the harp to soothe Saul's troubled spirit (16:14–23). When Saul rashly seeks to kill him because he is jealous of David's popularity and believes he will take over Saul's kingdom, David waits on God's timing to become the next king. He does not take matters into his own hands, even when he has the opportunity to kill Saul (chs. 24, 26). David seeks to serve God by fighting Judah's battles even when he is running from Saul (ch. 27). When Saul and Jonathan are killed in a battle against the Philistines, he does not rejoice but mourns their deaths (1 Sam. 31–2 Sam. 1). David is finally anointed king over Judah (2 Sam. 2) and then over all Israel (ch. 5).

32. David T. Tsumura translates the phrase as "a man of his choice." *The First Book of Samuel* (Grand Rapids: Eerdmans, 2007), 345.
33. Bergen (*1, 2 Samuel*, 151) gives both views as possible meanings of this phrase.

David continues to demonstrate his character when he becomes king. He consolidates the kingdom through the defeat of Israel's enemies (2 Sam. 8). When confronted with his sin—adultery with Bathsheba and the betrayal and murder of her husband, Uriah—David does not make excuses but confesses (2 Sam. 12; Ps. 51). When he is betrayed by Absalom and must leave Jerusalem, he leaves the ark behind. He submits himself to God's sovereign will concerning whether he will find favor in the eyes of the Lord and return to Jerusalem (2 Sam. 15:24–26). As he leaves the city, he humbly accepts the cursing of Shimei as from the Lord (16:5–14). When judgment from the Lord falls on the people because of David's sin in numbering them, he requests that the hand of God be against him and his house rather than against the innocent people (24:17). David had many flaws, but he was God's choice, and his heart was committed to the Lord.[34]

God's Covenant with David

David consolidated the kingdom by defeating his enemies, and God gave him rest on every side (2 Sam. 7:1). This rest was a fulfillment of a promise that God made to his people before they took over the land (Deut. 12:10). After the defeat of his enemies, David desired to build God a permanent house. God did not allow David to build a temple because of all the wars in which he participated. Instead, God promised that David's son would build a temple and that God would establish David's house. The Lord sovereignly established David's dynasty, and that dynasty would establish God's dwelling (2 Sam. 7:13), binding David's rule to his rule. God entered into a covenant with David and made promises concerning his descendants. This covenant established

---

34. David was very sincere in his repentance, but his life shows the devastating consequences that his sin brought on his family, in part by his unwillingness to discipline his sons (2 Sam. 12–20).

an enduring Davidic dynasty and changed the king's relationship to God in the unfolding of redemptive history.

The Terms of the Covenant

Although the word *covenant* is not used in 2 Samuel 7, Psalm 89:3 refers to God's promises as a covenant. The promises include the establishment of a kingdom through one of David's offspring. This descendant will build a house for the Lord, and the throne of his kingdom will endure forever. A father–son relationship will be established between God and the king. If this king commits iniquity, God will discipline him, but God's steadfast love will not depart from him as it did from Saul. The outcome of this covenant: David's house, kingdom, and throne will be established forever.

This covenant, like most others in Scripture, has conditional and unconditional elements.[35] The conditional element is that the king from David's line must live in obedience to God or he will experience God's discipline. The unconditional element is that God will not take his steadfast love away from the king, rejecting him and his descendants as God did with Saul. The covenant promises of an eternal kingdom and an eternal throne will be fulfilled. No amount of human disobedience will be able to hinder the fulfillment of God's promises to David.

The Outworking of the Covenant in History

Solomon is the initial fulfillment of the promises in the Davidic covenant. He is the descendant of David who built the first temple (1 Kings 7–8). If David can be described as the ideal king, Solomon's reign can be described as the ideal kingdom of peace and security. Many of God's promises to his people are

---

35. Bruce K. Waltke, "The Phenomenon of Conditionality within Unconditional Covenants," in *Israel's Apostasy and Restoration*, ed. Avraham Gileadi (Grand Rapids: Baker, 1988), 130–32. For more on the Davidic covenant, see O. Palmer Robertson, *The Christ of the Covenants* (Phillipsburg, NJ: Presbyterian and Reformed, 1980), 229–69.

initially fulfilled in Solomon's kingdom: the Abrahamic promise that the people would be as numerous as the sand on the seashore (Gen. 22:17; 1 Kings 4:20); the promise that God would give the land to Abraham's descendants (Gen. 12:7; 1 Kings 4:24); and the blessings of the Mosaic covenant—the kingdom is blessed with peace and abundant prosperity (Deut. 28:1–14; 1 Kings 4:25), and all the nations see God's blessings on Israel (Deut. 28:10; 1 Kings 4:34).

Solomon's kingdom is a partial restoration of the dominion human beings lost at the fall. There are possible allusions to Adam in the presentation of Solomon; in a partial way he functions as a second Adam.[36] Solomon is acclaimed king at Gihon (1 Kings 1:33, 38, 45), a water source on the slope below Jerusalem that bears the same name as one of the primeval rivers of Genesis 2:13. Solomon is urged to become a man (*ish*, אִישׁ) and keep (*shamar*, שָׁמַר) the charge of Yahweh (1 Kings 2:2–3). These concepts suggest a link with Genesis 2:15, where the first one to be called man (*ish*) is charged with keeping (*shamar*) the garden sanctuary as a priest guards the tabernacle (Num. 3:32; 2 Kings 12:9).[37] Solomon exercises dominion over God's creation by his understanding of animals and plants (1 Kings 4:33), as Adam did in the garden (Gen. 2:19–20). The difference is that God gives Solomon great wisdom to administer justice in the kingdom (1 Kings 3:9, 28). The administration of the law to ensure justice is important for government. The prospect of life is held out to Solomon, conditional on his obedience to the divine command (9:1–9), just as it was to Adam (Gen. 2:16–17).[38]

---

36. Many of the connections between Solomon and Adam come from John A. Davies, "Discerning between Good and Evil: Solomon as a New Adam in 1 Kings," *WTJ* 73, 1 (2011): 39–57.

37. For a discussion concerning whether David or Solomon had other priestly duties or acted as priests, see the Excursus. Davies discusses the roles of prophet, priest, and king in relationship to Solomon and concludes that if Solomon is portrayed as a priest, such a portrayal is highly irregular in terms of the Deuteronomic legislation.

38. The prayer of dedication for the temple contains many references to the curses of the covenant, such as defeat by the enemy (1 Kings 8:33–34; Deut. 28:25; Lev. 26:17),

The early period of Solomon's kingdom also fulfills the ideal of Israel's mission.[39] Israel was to live in the land that God gave her and obey the law, and then he would pour out his blessings so that nations would see and come to Jerusalem to give glory and honor to God. This mission is reflected in Solomon's prayer of dedication (1 Kings 8:41–43). It is exemplified in the visit of the queen of Sheba, who offered praise to Yahweh for such marvelous achievements (10:9), and in the statement that the whole world sought an audience with Solomon (v. 24). Other nations and kings brought their wealth to Jerusalem (vv. 11–12, 25). Israel was at the height of success with the fulfillment of the promises of God.

The early reign of Solomon manifested the blessings of a righteous kingdom (Psalm 72). And yet there are hints of trouble that culminate in 1 Kings 10–11.[40] The decline of Solomon's kingdom is directly related to the warnings given to kings in Deuteronomy 17:14–20. Solomon accumulated wealth (Deut. 17:17; 1 Kings 10:14–29), he accumulated horses (Deut. 17:16; 1 Kings 10:26–29), and he accumulated wives (Deut. 17:17; 1 Kings 11:1). His intermarriage with foreign women led to idolatry. Solomon's heart was turned away from the Lord, and he worshiped foreign gods (1 Kings 11:1–8). The results to his kingdom were devastating. God raised up adversaries from other nations (vv. 9–25), and he decided to tear the kingdom of Israel into two parts. He saved one tribe for the line of David but promised to give ten tribes to Jeroboam (vv. 31–35).

Rehoboam, son of Solomon, foolishly followed his young advisers and promised the people that his reign would be harder than Solomon's. The people rebelled, and the kingdom was

no rain (1 Kings 8:35–36; Deut. 28:23–24; Lev. 26:19–20), and exile (1 Kings 8:46–50; Deut. 28:36–37, 41; Lev. 26:33).

39. Israel's mission is discussed in chapter 1.

40. For a discussion of the negative aspects of Solomon's kingdom, see Yong Ho Jeon, "The Retroactive Re-evaluation Technique with Pharaoh's Daughter and the Nature of Solomon's Corruption in 1 Kings 1–12," *TynBul* 62, 1 (2011): 15–40.

divided. The history of the northern and southern kingdoms was a history of decline. No good kings ruled in the northern kingdom because they all followed the sin of Jeroboam, who set up his own worship centers to keep his people from going south to worship at Jerusalem. The northern kingdom fell to the Assyrians in 722 B.C. Some good kings, who sought to follow God, reigned in the southern kingdom, particularly Hezekiah and Josiah. But most did not follow God, and the people also broke God's covenant. The southern kingdom fell to Babylon in 587 B.C. The kings as shepherds of God's people bore a large part of the responsibility for the judgment of God against his people (Jer. 23; Ezek. 34:1–16).

The Promise of a Coming King

The covenant with David partially fulfills the previous promises for One who would come to rule Israel (Gen. 3:15; 49:10–12; Num. 24:17). Deuteronomy 17:14–20 had specified how a king was to function in Israel. The passage emphasizes that the king was to be an Israelite—not a foreigner, but a brother to his companions (v. 15). He was to obey the law so that his heart was not lifted above his brothers (v. 20). The king was a common Israelite ruling in a context of covenant equality with other leaders.[41] The covenant with David does not deny what Deuteronomy 17 teaches, but it elevates the status of the king, who is now in a father–son relationship with God (2 Sam. 7:14). During the exodus, Israel was called God's firstborn son (Ex. 4:22), and now the king of Israel has the status of son. The king as son represents the people to God and takes on certain roles that were not clearly the role of the king in Deuteronomy 17, uniting in his person things that were kept separate.[42] The administration of justice is divided

41. Christopher Wright, *Deuteronomy* (Peabody, MA: Hendrickson, 1996), 210.
42. J. G. McConville, *Deuteronomy* (Downers Grove, IL: InterVarsity Press, 2002), 295, 306.

among various groups in Deuteronomy 16–18, but it becomes the particular responsibility of the king (Ps. 72).

The king also took on certain responsibilities for worship. He supported the true worship of God and—in certain situations—had a role in offering sacrifices. David brought the ark to Jerusalem, wore a linen ephod, offered burnt offerings and peace offerings, and blessed the people in the name of the Lord (2 Sam. 6). This was a special occasion, and there is no evidence that David regularly offered sacrifices. He made extensive preparations for building the temple, which Solomon completed. Evidence shows that Solomon offered sacrifices regularly, but at Gibeon and not at the altar at Jerusalem (1 Kings 3:3–5).[43] He did offer sacrifices at Jerusalem after the Lord appeared to him in a dream in which he was promised great wealth and wisdom (v. 15). Solomon built the temple and dedicated it to the Lord in a great ceremony (ch. 8). The ark was brought to the temple with many sacrifices offered (vv. 4–5, 62–64), and Solomon offered a blessing to the people (v. 14), a prayer of dedication (vv. 22–53), and a benediction (vv. 54–61). The elevated status of the king gave him certain privileges related to worship and the offering of sacrifices. This did not mean, however, that the kings became priests or that the establishment of a special royal priesthood combined the roles of the king and priest (see the Excursus). There were clear limits throughout the Old Testament on what the king could do in the holy areas of the temple. When the ark was brought to Jerusalem in 1 Kings 8, the priests brought it into the Most Holy Place. When Uzziah tried to offer incense on the

43. Many reasons are given for why Solomon offered sacrifices at Gibeon. There are political reasons, since Gibeon was the natural hub of conflict between Israel and Judah. It was also home to the largest high place in the country. August H. Konkel, *1 & 2 Kings* (Grand Rapids: Zondervan, 2006), 78. Second Chronicles 1:5–6 explains that the ark was at Jerusalem and that the Tent of Meeting and bronze altar were at Gibeon. Paul R. House, *1, 2 Kings* (Nashville: Broadman & Holman, 1995), 109. Before the temple was built, sacrifices were offered at a number of places.

altar in the temple, he was struck with leprosy because only the priests were allowed to offer incense (2 Chron. 26:16–21). A clear line divided the role of the kings and the role of the priests in the regular worship of God. Kings could support the worship at the temple and on certain special occasions could offer sacrifices, but they were limited in what they could do.

Another way in which the covenant with David elevated the role of the king was its promises that the kingdom of David and his throne would be established forever (2 Sam. 7:16–17). This expectation became important when the southern kingdom fell and there was no king ruling over Israel. Also, the terminology of the covenant lends itself to being understood as referring to a coming eschatological ruler, who will not only rule over Israel but rule over the nations forever. The failure of kingship at key points in Israel's history leads to the prospect of a coming ruler who will be faithful to the Lord. At times this ruler takes on characteristics that go beyond what might be said of a purely human ruler. For example, when King Ahaz refuses to trust Yahweh and rejects the offer of a sign, there follows a series of prophecies concerning a coming ruler. God himself gives the sign of a virgin who will bear a son whose name will be Immanuel, "God with us." This Child will embody the very presence of God. Isaiah 9 speaks of the birth of a son who will sit on the throne of David and establish his kingdom through justice and righteousness. The character of this Child is emphasized by the name given to him. He will be called *Wonderful Counselor* because his plans will not fail (unlike King Ahaz's plans). He will be called *Mighty God*. This phrase is used of Yahweh, the Holy One of Israel, in Isaiah 10:21–23. This son not only will embody the presence of God but will take on the character of deity.[44] He will be called

---

44. For commentaries on Isaiah arguing that these names refer to the character of the coming ruler, see those by Edward J. Young, J. A. Motyer, John N. Oswalt, John L. Mackay, and Gary V. Smith. Mackay answers the views that these terms are really describing God, not the coming king, or that the king described is a descendant of

Everlasting Father because as a King he will be the benevolent protector of his people. And finally, he will be called *Prince of Peace* because he will establish peace.

The character of this King's reign is described in Isaiah 11. The One who will establish the kingdom is described as "a shoot from the stump of Jesse, and a branch from his roots"[45] (v. 1). The effectiveness of his reign is due to an outpouring of the Spirit on him. In verse 2 there are four uses of the word *Spirit*, denoting the source of this ruler's wisdom, knowledge, and fear of the Lord. This King will rule in righteousness by which he will judge the poor, decide with equity for the meek, and slay the wicked with the breath of his mouth (v. 4). The results of his rule reflect Eden-like conditions of harmony and peace among the animals and between animals and human beings. There may be an allusion to Genesis 3:15 with the child playing over the hole of the cobra without fear of harm.[46] The earth will be filled with the knowledge of the Lord, and the nations will submit themselves to the Lord.

The Psalms emphasize the role of a king and also keep alive the hope for a coming ruler. Certain royal psalms in the first three

---

Ahaz. *A Study Commentary on Isaiah*, vol. 1, *Chapters 1–39* (Darlington, UK: Evangelical Press, 2008), 241–42.

Oswalt interacts with the view that these names are throne names related to the various gods, as in Egypt. *The Book of Isaiah: Chapters 1–39* (Grand Rapids: Eerdmans, 1986), 246; see also Gary V. Smith, *Isaiah 1–39* (Nashville: Broadman & Holman, 2007), 240.

45. For a discussion of the term *branch* (*nezer*) and its possible connection to Matthew 2:23, see Mackay, *A Study Commentary on Isaiah*, 290. After the condemnation of the kings of Israel in Jeremiah 22:1–23:4, God promises to raise up for David a righteous branch (*tsemakh*); for a discussion of this term, see John L. Mackay, *Jeremiah: An Introduction and Commentary*, vol. 2, *Chapters 21–52* (Ross-shire, UK: Mentor, 2004), 50–54.

46. Commentaries on Isaiah that understand Isaiah 11 to reference a return of Eden-like conditions include those of Edward J. Young, J. A. Motyer, John L. Mackay, and Gary V. Smith. Young answers objections brought by those who argue against the literal interpretation of the passage, favoring a figurative view that the animals stand for the nations. *The Book of Isaiah*, vol. 1, *Chapters 1–18* (Grand Rapids: Eerdmans, 1965), 390–91. Of course, the nations are impacted by renewal brought by the reign of the Messiah (Isa. 11:11–16).

books of the Psalter focus on key elements of his rule. Psalm 2 emphasizes that God's reign will be established through his anointed king. The king's special relationship to God is emphasized in verse 7: "You are my Son; today I have begotten you." Sonship is not a physical or mythical relationship; it is a legal relationship between God and the king, which ensures the king's victory. He will one day rule the world. The reign of a righteous king and the results of his reign are given in Psalm 72. It includes the establishment of justice, dominion over the nations, and an abundance of blessings for the people under his reign. In Psalm 89 the promises of the Davidic covenant are highlighted, with God's faithfulness being the foundation. The Davidic king is called the firstborn (v. 27), a term that refers to his position as "the highest of the kings of the earth." The lament at the end of the psalm is shocking to the reader in light of the early strong emphasis on God's faithfulness to the covenant promises (vv. 38–45). The humiliation of the king is described in these verses. The problem is not God's faithfulness but the unfaithfulness of the anointed king. The questions at the end of the psalm (vv. 46–51) call upon God to show again his favor to David and establish his covenant promises.[47]

Books 4 and 5 of the Psalter reflect the exilic and postexilic situations of the people. Book 3 ended with the kingship in trouble (Ps. 89), and Book 4 begins with a psalm of Moses, taking the people back to their foundation as a nation. God's steadfast love has not been totally removed from the people (92:1–2), and even if the human kingship is in trouble, Yahweh still reigns (Pss. 93–100). Book 4 ends with a cry that God would save his people from exile (106:47). This is answered at the beginning of Book 5 (107:1–3), which puts psalms in groups that emphasize what is important to the postexilic community, including worship (Pss. 111–118;

---

47. For more on these psalms and the structure of the Psalter, see Richard P. Belcher Jr., *The Messiah and the Psalms* (Ross-shire, UK: Christian Focus, 2006), and O. Palmer Robertson, *The Flow of the Psalms: Discovering Their Structure and Theology* (Phillipsburg, NJ: P&R Publishing, 2015).

120–134), the law (Ps. 119), and kingship (Pss. 108–110; 138–145). The Psalter ends in a fireworks of praise as it recounts the destiny of the righteous who celebrate God's victory (Pss. 146–150).

The two groups of Davidic psalms in Book 5 remind the people of the kind of king they need. Psalm 110 is an important psalm that sets forth the coming King as One who sits at the right hand of God and who is a Priest according to the order of Melchizedek. The coming ruler will be both a King and a Priest. It is difficult to apply the role of a priest–king to any Israelite ruler. The Israelite king supported the worship at the temple and even on some occasions offered sacrifices himself, but there were strict limits on what the king could do in the sanctuary (2 Chron. 26:16–21). It is difficult to see any king in the history of Israel fulfilling the role laid out in Psalm 110. The King who will sit at the right hand of God and be a Priest according to the order of Melchizedek is a coming ruler who will combine these two roles in his reign. How such a King could also be humble (Zech. 9:9–10) and experience humiliation (Ps. 89), in addition to being highly exalted, is a puzzle that will not be solved until the One comes who is able to accomplish all the purposes of God.

Excursus: Was There a Royal Priesthood in Israel?

Passages in the Old Testament present the kings of Israel acting as priests. Other passages seem to identify the sons of David as priests. How are these to be understood? Did a royal priesthood related to David and his descendants develop in Israel? If it existed, what did this mean for the kings of Israel in the nation's worship?

The Argument for a Royal Priesthood in Israel

The evidence for a royal priesthood comes from how certain passages present the actions of the king in relationship to worship and how certain passages seem to identify David and his sons as priests (2 Sam. 8:18). Second Samuel 20:23–26 identifies Ira the Jairite as the priest to David in addition to the official Levitical priests Zadok and Abiathar. First Kings 4:1–5 also mentions Zadok and Abiathar, but also identifies Zabud the son of Nathan as a priest and the king's friend. Some argue from these texts that there were priests in early Israel who were connected to the royal house but were not of the Levitical order. The function they performed is not entirely clear.[48] Based on David's role in bringing the ark to Jerusalem (2 Sam. 6) and the roles of Zadok and Abiathar during this period, the conclusion is drawn that David was the chief sacrificial and priestly intermediary between Yahweh and the people during his reign. The same could be said about Adonijah (1 Kings 1:9, 18) and Solomon (chs. 3, 8), who undertook similar priestly activities.[49]

The priestly model for these kings is not the Levitical order but the order of Melchizedek taken from Psalm 110. This psalm sets forth the prototype of the messianic High Priest. The priestly activities of David and Solomon hold special significance in light of this psalm. These connections establish that there was a strong sense of royal–priestly ideology that existed in early Israel. The order of Melchizedek serves as a prototype in which David and Solomon are thought to act as priests.[50] In fact, David himself is the link between Melchizedek and Jesus because he is the subject of Psalm 110. David is a royal priest, and he is the precursor in a line of priests that finds its fullest and perfect expression in Jesus.[51]

48. Carl Amerding, "Were David's Sons Really Priests?," in *Current Issues in Biblical and Patristic Interpretation*, ed. Gerald F. Hawthorne (Grand Rapids: Eerdmans, 1975), 75–76.
49. Ibid., 82–83.
50. Ibid., 84.
51. Eugene H. Merrill, "Royal Priesthood: An Old Testament Messianic Motif," *BSac* 150 (January–March 1993): 53.

Key to this understanding of Psalm 110 is the identification of the one addressed at the beginning of the psalm as "my Lord." Those who understand the psalm to be speaking directly of Christ see *my Lord* as referring to Jesus. The problem with this view is that Psalm 110 would then lack a clear occasion and would not have relevance for its own historical context. The *my Lord* could be referring to David, whose priesthood is being described in verses 2-4. This priesthood operates outside the boundaries of the normal cultic sphere. In this view David functions as a messianic type not only regarding the kingship but also regarding the priesthood. He fills both roles and discharges both responsibilities simultaneously. The priesthood according to the order of Melchizedek is modeled by David, who is also declared to be a priest after this order and who exercised this priesthood from time to time, as did his dynastic successors.[52]

Royal Priesthood: Strictly Messianic

Others argue that the priesthood according to Melchizedek is not historically manifested in any king of Israel but is fulfilled only in the priesthood of Jesus Christ. This view takes Psalm 110 as directly messianic.[53] It is a psalm of David, so he is the one speaking in the psalm and he is not the subject of the psalm.[54] David writes that "the LORD" (Yahweh) addressed someone that David describes as "my Lord." Thus three people are referred to in this verse: (1) Yahweh, (2) the sovereign Lord, and (3) David, who claims to have a close relationship with the sovereign Lord.[55]

52. Ibid., 54-58, 61.
53. For an analysis of how the different historical settings impact the interpretation of Psalm 110, see Belcher, *Messiah and the Psalms*, 143-48.
54. F. Delitzsch, "Psalms," in *Commentary on the Old Testament*, ed. C. F. Keil and F. Delitzsch (Grand Rapids: Eerdmans, 1978), 5:188; see also Michael Rydelnik, *The Messianic Hope: Is the Hebrew Bible Really Messianic?* (Nashville: B&H Academic, 2010), 165-68.
55. Gerard Van Groningen, *Messianic Revelation in the Old Testament* (Grand Rapids: Baker, 1990), 391. See also Allan Harman, *Psalms*, vol. 2, *Psalms 73-150* (Ross-shire, UK: Christian Focus, 2011), 793.

The king of Israel is not being addressed by Psalm 110:1. The king sits on the throne of Yahweh as a representative of God, the true King. The one addressed as "my Lord" sits at the right hand of God, an exaltation to a special participation in God's reign.[56] The New Testament clearly identifies David as this psalm's author, not its subject (Matt. 22:43–44; Mark 12:36; Luke 20:42; Acts 2:34).[57]

Other factors argue against the view that David the king is being established as a royal priest. One would assume that a priest according to the order of Melchizedek would not be hindered in fulfilling any of the priestly roles, including the privilege of sacrificing in the sanctuary and receiving the tithes of the people.[58] Thus, if David had no claim on the tithes of the priests like Melchizedek, and if Davidic kings were denied the authority to offer sacrifices, how can David be called a priest after the order of Melchizedek?[59] King Uzziah was prohibited from offering incense to the Lord on the altar inside the Holy Place because only the priests were consecrated to offer incense. When Uzziah persisted, leprosy broke out on his forehead. This separation of the kingly and priestly privileges was so important that he remained a leper to the day of his death (2 Chron. 26:16–21). To establish a royal priesthood of David requires evidence not that the king played a priestly part in certain festival rites, but that he ordinarily exercised the priest's functions and was as truly the priest as he was the king.[60]

56. Delitzsch, "Psalms," 5:189.

57. Merrill ("Royal Priesthood," 54) recognizes that this is the view of the NT, and yet it does not affect his view that David is the subject of the psalm and not the author.

58. This is especially true if Melchizedek in Genesis 14 is a high priest (Delitzsch, "Psalms," 193). Bergen argues that (1) David and his family line attained the priestly status "in the order of Melchizedek," and (2) as king of Jerusalem, David would become a priest of Yahweh but would still be prohibited from performing certain priestly functions reserved for the Aaronic priesthood. *1, 2 Samuel*, 332. This view better fits the OT evidence, but see below for the view that the priesthood "according to the order of Melchizedek" is a unique priesthood.

59. Delitzsch, "Psalms," 5:193.

60. M. J. Paul, "The Order of Melchizedek (Ps 110:4 and Heb 7:3)," *WTJ* 49, 1 (1987): 197–98.

It is also important to recognize that the priesthood according to Melchizedek in Genesis 14 is a type of a completely different order from the Aaronic priesthood. As a type, it looks forward to the priesthood of Christ, who ministers as a Priest at the heavenly sanctuary. If the priesthood of Melchizedek is another kind, it would not be a priesthood that could be fulfilled in any Israelite king, even if he offered sacrifices in the temple in the Most Holy Place on the Day of Atonement.[61] The priesthood of Melchizedek is a type of a heavenly priesthood that only Jesus can fulfill (Heb. 7:15–19).[62]

If Psalm 110 does not establish the Davidic king as a priest according to the order of Melchizedek, then how can David's actions—and those of other kings—in offering sacrifices be explained? It was in the best interest of the king to ensure proper worship. This was true in the ancient Near East and became true in Israel with the elevated status of the king as adopted son of God in the Davidic covenant. Once David had consolidated his kingdom, he desired to build God a permanent temple. He prepared for the building of the temple, and Solomon completed the work. But even in the ancient Near East, there was a clear distinction between the administrative royal priest (the king) and the functional cultic priests. The latter were responsible for the cultic service at the temple. The former had only an administrative role; it did not include performing services in the temple. The king was responsible for the organization and administration of state worship. He was involved with organizing the priesthood and arranging for the construction of temples and financing sacrifices on behalf of the throne and the state.[63] If the king could

---

61. Van Groningen, *Messianic Revelation*, 395.

62. Paul ("The Order of Melchizedek," 203) argues that the eternal nature of the priesthood of Melchizedek is concerned with a single person, not with many descendants.

63. Herbert W. Bateman IV, Darrell L. Bock, and Gordon H. Johnston, *Jesus the Messiah* (Grand Rapids: Kregel, 2012), 97–98. This work argues that David was a royal priest,

not officiate in the temple in the regular worship, his role was limited to special occasions.[64]

Several passages seem to argue for the existence of priests outside the Aaronic priesthood; these might support the view that David and his descendants are priests according to the order of Melchizedek. The most obvious passage is 2 Samuel 8:18; there, in a list of royal officials, the statement is made that "David's sons were priests." This text seems to be fairly clear, but the parallel text in 1 Chronicles 18:17 throws doubt on its meaning. Both verses state that Benaiah, the son of Jehoiada, was over the Cherethites and Pelethites, and both mention the role of David's sons. First Chronicles 18:17 does not call David's sons *priests* but calls them "chief officials in the service of the king." This ambiguity allows for the possibility that *priests* in 2 Samuel 8:18 has a different meaning.[65] In 1 Kings 4:5, two of Nathan's sons are given important roles. Azariah is over the officers so that he supervised the district officers (vv. 7–19). Zabud is called a priest and the king's friend. These terms could refer to the role of special counsel to the king.[66] The same could be said for the statement in 2 Samuel 20:23–26 that "Ira Jairite was also David's

but does not take into account the implications of the king's limitations in worship.

64. Roland de Vaux, *Ancient Israel: Its Life and Institutions* (Grand Rapids: Eerdmans, 1961), 114; Patrick Miller, *The Religion of Ancient Israel* (Louisville, KY: Westminster John Knox Press, 2000), 194. The historical period between the tabernacle existing at Shiloh with Eli as priest and the dedication of the temple by Solomon gives evidence of fluidity concerning the offering of sacrifices by Samuel and Solomon (Paul, "The Order of Melchizedek," 196–97).

65. Gordon J. Wenham argues for emending the text from *priest* (כהנים) to *administrators* (שכנים). "Were David's Sons Priests?," *ZAW* 87 (1975): 79–82. An emendation of the text is not necessary. Others see the role of David's sons as court chaplains. David Firth, *1 & 2 Samuel* (Downers Grove, IL: InterVarsity Press, 2009), 399.

66. House, *1, 2 Kings*, 115. Keil and Delitzsch understand "the king's friend" in 1 Kings 4:5 to be an explanation of the word *priest*. Thus 2 Samuel 8:18 is referring to the king's confidential advisers. Others argue that the fact that David's sons are not mentioned in this text could be evidence that their role as priests was temporary. Roger L. Omanson and John E. Ellington, *Handbook on First and Second Books of Samuel*, 2 vols. (New York: United Bible Societies, 2001), 2:790.

priest." If these men are not royal advisers but serve as priests to David, it does not prove that they are of the order of Melchizedek. Several orders of non-Levitical priests, even if they do exist in Israel,[67] do not establish a priestly order of Melchizedek that is hereditary in the Davidic line. Second Samuel 20:23–26 provides a second listing of key administrative officials under David. This list probably represents those who served near the end of his reign.[68] Ira the Jairite is listed as David's priest. It is possible that the omission of David's sons as priests means that he reduced the significance of their priestly role during his reign and that these duties were assumed by Ira.[69] Whatever one concludes from these texts, the scriptural evidence is too ambiguous to draw definite conclusions about a priestly order according to Melchizedek that historically existed in Israel's history.

Study Questions

1. What impact does sin have on the exercise of dominion? Trace the development in Genesis through Numbers of the One who will come to rule.
2. How did the role of the kings in Israel differ from the kings of the ancient Near East? How do we account for this significant difference?
3. What is the basic argument of the book of Judges? How does this shed light on the role of the king in Israel?
4. What was wrong about the people's request for a king in 1 Samuel 8? How might this instruct the church as she relates to the surrounding culture?
5. Why does God reject Saul as king over Israel? What does this teach us about God's priorities?

67. Amerding, "Were David's Sons Really Priests?," 76.
68. Bergen, *1, 2 Samuel*, 438.
69. Ibid., 439.

6. What promises did God make to David in the Davidic covenant? What is the significance of this covenant?

7. What is meant by the term *royal priesthood*? What are the arguments for and against the existence of a royal priesthood in Israel?

7

CHRIST AS KING IN HIS
HUMILIATION AND EXALTATION

THE ROLE OF DOMINION was clearly given to human beings in Genesis 1:26–28. The fall into sin made dominion difficult, but its continuing role was evident in Israel's conquest of Canaan and in the establishment of the king to rule according to God's law. The king was to lead the nation to fulfill the mission that God had given her to be a light to the nations.[1] The failure of Israel's kings to live in obedience to God led to the hope of a coming King, who would properly lead God's people in righteousness to establish an everlasting kingdom (see chapter 6). The Jewish people of Jesus' day had certain expectations concerning the coming King. They were looking for a king like David, a warrior king, who would conquer the Roman government and establish Israel as a great nation as in the days of David and Solomon. The problem with Jesus was that he did not fit the mold of a king who would lead Israel into revolt against the Romans. Much

---

1. Chapter 1 discusses the mission of Israel in light of the roles of prophet, priest, and king.

of his teaching advocated submission to the authorities (Matt. 5:38–42; 26:51–54; Mark 12:13–17), and he seemed to speak against the religious leaders of the Jewish people more than the leaders of Rome (Matt. 23). Jesus also talked a lot about his coming suffering, which the disciples did not understand (Mark 8:31–33; 9:30–32) because it did not fit with their notions of the coming Messiah and his kingdom. The expectations of the disciples were not completely wrong. The timing of their expectation of a conquering king must be adjusted, and the definition of the kingdom that Christ came to establish needed to be understood. Part of the purpose of Jesus' earthly ministry was to help the disciples understand his mission and the nature of his kingdom.

Jesus as King during His Earthly Ministry

The disciples did not understand the nature of Jesus' kingship partly because suffering and kingship do not easily fit together. A suffering king seems to be a contradiction. How can someone exercise rule and authority through suffering? But the rule of Jesus is demonstrated in several ways during his earthly ministry of humiliation.

Dominion over Creation

Part of Jesus' mission was to show that he had the power to restore creation. He demonstrated this power through his miracles. He calmed the wind and the storm at sea, showing his rule over the elements of creation (Matt. 8:23–27; Mark 4:35–41; Luke 8:22–25). Jesus rebuked the wind, showing his authority over it (Luke 8:24). The disciples were amazed and asked the question, "What sort of man is this, that even winds and sea obey him?" (Matt. 8:27).[2]

2. This incident shows Jesus' humanity in his sleeping during the storm and Jesus' royal rule in his power over the wind and the sea.

Jesus also demonstrated his rule over creation when he healed many people of illness and disease. Matthew, Mark, and Luke all record miracles of healing at the beginning of Jesus' ministry. These healings generated a lot of interest in him. Great crowds followed him (Matt. 4:25; Mark 1:29–34), and opposition began to form against him (Mark 2:1–12). These miracles were an outpouring of great blessing from God and indicated that he was at work. It was natural for questions to arise concerning Jesus' identity in light of his power to bring great blessing into people's lives. Jesus fed the five thousand, and the people responded by wanting to make him king (John 6:1–15). They saw the connection between material blessing and the righteous reign of the king to come.[3] Jesus knew their plans and withdrew from them. Their perception of kingship was not in line with the kind of King that Jesus came to be in his humiliation. These miracles, however, were evidence of his power to restore creation as part of his mission.

Dominion over the Demons

Jesus did not come to be a mere dispenser of material blessings. The blessings that came through his miracles gave evidence of a spiritual battle that he participated in as King. Many of his miracles were related to his power over the spiritual forces of wickedness represented by Satan and his demons. Near the beginning of Jesus' ministry, he healed a man with an unclean spirit (Mark 1:21–28; Luke 4:31–37). The demon clearly expressed his conflict with Jesus, and that Jesus' coming would have an impact on his own world of demonic activity. He asked Jesus, "Have you come to destroy us?" This question recognized the

---

3. Richard P. Belcher Jr., *The Messiah and the Psalms* (Ross-shire, UK: Christian Focus, 2006), 138–39. Jesus' first miracle in John's Gospel, turning water into wine (2:1–12), is not just a good gesture to help out at a wedding. His statement to his mother in verse 4 shows implications in this miracle that relate to his ministry. The wine is a reminder of the great blessings that will come through Jesus, even a transformation of creation, as prophesied in Amos 9:11–15, where abundance of wine is a sign of great future blessing.

true source of Jesus' origin and the true nature of Jesus' mission. The demon also confessed the true identity of Jesus as the Holy One of God. He correctly identified Jesus as his great opponent who had come to defeat the forces of wickedness.[4] Jesus drove the unclean spirit out of the man, and the people responded with amazement that Jesus was able to command the unclean spirits and that they had obeyed him (Mark 1:27). This incident caused Jesus' fame to spread and led to people's bringing the sick to be healed. He also cast out many demons (vv. 29–32). Mark has an interesting comment that Jesus would not allow the demons to speak because they knew him (v. 34), even proclaiming that "you are the Son of God" (Luke 4:41). There was danger that the people would misunderstand the true nature of Jesus' ministry before he had an opportunity to explain his mission.

Many of Jesus' works demonstrated his power in the spiritual realm. He healed the paralytic to show that he had the power to forgive sins (Mark 2:1–12). Jesus raised several people from the dead to demonstrate his power over death. He raised Jairus's daughter from the dead to show that, in his presence, death is like sleep from which he has the power to wake people up (Matt. 9:22–26; Mark 5:35–43; Luke 8:49–58).[5] He raised the widow's son from the dead, a miracle that people saw as evidence that God had visited his people (Luke 7:11–17). Luke follows this incident with John the Baptist's question whether Jesus was the One who was to come. Jesus highlighted how his ministry aligned with the coming One described in Isaiah 61, including "the dead are raised up" (Luke 7:22). His greatest confrontation with death, apart from his own death on the cross, comes in John 11 when he raised

---

4. William Hendriksen, *Exposition of the Gospel according to Luke* (Grand Rapids: Baker, 1978), 265.

5. The comparison of death to sleep does not mean that the girl did not die. Death is also compared to sleep in the case of Lazarus, who was raised after being dead four days (John 11:11, 39–44). The comparison means that death is temporary. Both incidents also teach that faith in Jesus is the way to overcome death.

Lazarus from the dead. Jesus was deeply moved in his spirit and greatly troubled at Lazarus's death. He even wept (vv. 33–35). It is not the weeping people but the tomb that evoked these intense emotions of aversion and sorrow.[6] He was staring death in the face. Calvin comments, "Christ does not come to the sepulcher as an idle spectator, but like a wrestler preparing for the contest. Therefore no wonder that he groans again, for the violent tyranny of death that He had to overcome stands before His eyes."[7]

Jesus used Lazarus's death to teach about spiritual life and the resurrection. He proclaimed, "I am the resurrection and the life" (John 11:25) and went on to explain what he meant in verses 25 and 26. The statement *I am the resurrection* is explained by "whoever believes in me, though he die, yet shall he live." Someone who believes in Jesus will be resurrected to life after death. The statement *and the life* (with the *I am* implied) is explained by "and everyone who lives and believes in me shall never die." Someone can now experience the life Jesus offers by believing in him. This life is greater than death and will overcome death.[8] Jesus demonstrated his statements' truth by raising Lazarus after he had been dead four days.

The Kingdom of God

Matthew, Mark, and Luke mention the basic message of Jesus at the beginning of his ministry. Mark 1:14–15 states, "Jesus came into Galilee, proclaiming the gospel of God, and saying,

6. Herman N. Ridderbos, *The Gospel of John: A Theological Commentary* (Grand Rapids: Eerdmans), 402.

7. John Calvin, "John 1–11," in *Calvin's Commentaries*, vol. 17 (Grand Rapids: Baker, 1996), 442.

8. Ridderbos (*John*, 396) explains verses 25b through 26 this way: "Vs. 25b refers to death in the natural sense and to living in the sense of eternal life. 'Lives' in vs. 26a, on the other hand, refers to natural human existence, while 'never die' refers to the eternal life that natural death can neither prevent nor affect." The first statement refers to the deceased believer who will live and the second statement to the one who lives in faith and will not die.

'The time is fulfilled, and the kingdom of God is at hand; repent and believe in the gospel'" (see also Matt. 4:17).[9] This proclamation of the kingdom is followed by casting out demons and by healing many who are sick (Mark 1:21–34). After these miracles, the people sought Jesus and did not want him to leave their area. His response was: "I must preach the good news of the kingdom of God to the other towns as well; for I was sent for this purpose" (Luke 4:43). His miracles and his power over creation and the demons is evidence of the kingdom that he had come to establish.

Jewish Expectations of the Kingdom. Part of the reason why Jesus told the demons to keep quiet about his identity is that people would misunderstand the nature of his mission in light of their expectations of what the coming King would accomplish. The Old Testament depicts the role and mission of the One who will come in several different ways, and it is difficult to put these threads together into a whole picture. The Old Testament speaks of a coming King who will defeat the enemies of God's people and establish a rule of righteousness and peace (Isa. 9:6–7; 11:1–9). It speaks of a coming King–Priest who will be used by God to execute judgment on the nations (Ps. 110:4–6).[10] It also speaks of a Servant who will suffer on behalf of the people (Isa. 52:13–53:12) and a King who will come in humility to Jerusalem (Zech. 9:9). It is difficult to comprehend how the suffering and the conquering fit together into a unified picture. The nature of the kingdom and Jesus' mission begins to make sense of these Old Testament threads so that a comprehensive picture emerges.

9. There is virtually no difference between the phrase *kingdom of God* and *kingdom of heaven*. Matthew uses the phrase *kingdom of heaven* in line with the fixed Jewish linguistic usage in which the name of God was usually avoided. Herman N. Ridderbos, *The Coming of the Kingdom* (Philadelphia: Presbyterian and Reformed, 1962), 19.

10. For the view that Qumran expected two Messiahs, a kingly and a priestly, see Craig A. Evans, "The Messiah in the Dead Sea Scrolls," in *Israel's Messiah in the Bible and the Dead Sea Scrolls*, ed. Richard S. Hess and M. Daniel Carroll R. (Grand Rapids: Baker, 2003), 85–108.

The people of Jesus' day were expecting a king like David who would destroy their enemies, including the Roman government, and establish Israel as a great nation. They were expecting a powerful king who would establish a political kingdom. The reign of such a king would impact the nations. The nature of Jesus' kingdom—at least the one he came to establish during his earthly ministry—did not fit their expectations.[11] The nature of his kingdom can be seen in the passages where Jesus specifically mentions that the kingdom of God was in their midst through his ministry. His power to cast out demons caused his popularity to grow. They were amazed when they saw the before-and-after condition of a man who had been demon-possessed. This authority leads to the question of Jesus' identity, with people raising the issue, "Can this be the son of David?" (Matt. 12:23). Earlier in Matthew, two blind men seeking healing cried out to Jesus as he passed by, "Have mercy on us, son of David" (9:27). The term *son of David* is used in reference to Jesus' power to heal and to cast out demons. Evidence shows that *son of David* had become a formal designation of the Messiah.[12] When the Pharisees were asked to identify the lineage of the Christ (Messiah), they responded, "The son of David" (22:42). The identification of the Messiah with the son of David shows that the people expected a king to arise like David to sit on the throne of David.

The Pharisees could not allow a connection between Jesus and the son of David to stand, so they attributed his power to cast out demons to Beelzebul, the prince of the demons. In other words, Jesus' power to cast out demons came from the prince of the demons himself. Jesus responded by highlighting the absurdity of their statement, arguing that if he cast out demons by the power of the prince of demons, then the kingdom of the demons was divided against itself. Satan was casting out Satan. A divided

---

11. Ridderbos, *Kingdom*, 35.
12. Herman N. Ridderbos, *Matthew* (Grand Rapids: Zondervan, 1987), 190.

kingdom would not stand. The true source of his power came from the Spirit of God. Jesus was in conflict with the world of Satan and came to plunder his house (Matt. 12:29). Jesus came to battle Satan and to restore what Satan had distorted and destroyed. To do this, Jesus had to restrict and overcome the power of Satan, as he had done in casting out demons. This hostility resulted from the entrance of sin into the world (Gen. 3:15). Jesus was reasserting the power of God over the demons through his ministry. In fact, through Jesus' ministry the kingdom of God had come.

The Present Reality of the Kingdom. If the kingdom of God is a present reality available through Jesus, it can be entered immediately. Jesus tells the chief priests and elders that tax collectors and prostitutes are entering the kingdom of God before them. This statement must have come as a shock to the Jewish leaders, since they despised both groups. The tax collectors and the prostitutes are part of God's kingdom, but the Jewish leaders are not part of that kingdom. How could this be? The issue comes down to believing God's message. Those who are entering the kingdom of God believed the message of John the Baptist, but the Jewish leaders did not (Matt. 21:32). John pointed the way to Jesus, and ultimately a person's relationship to the kingdom will be determined by his or her relationship to Jesus. For one to enter the kingdom, one must be born again by believing in Jesus through the power of the Spirit (John 3:3, 6, 15).

If the kingdom of God is present through the ministry of Jesus, and people can enter it through faith in him, what is the nature of this kingdom that he came to establish? The word *kingdom* is generally associated with a territory or realm over which a king rules. It can also refer to the authority and sovereignty exercised by a king.[13] This meaning is seen in Ezra 8:1, which speaks of the *kingdom* or reign of Artaxerxes (see also 2 Chron.

---

13. George Eldon Ladd, *The Gospel of the Kingdom* (Grand Rapids: Eerdmans, 1959), 19; Ridderbos, *Kingdom*, 24–25.

12:1, which refers to the *rule* of Rehoboam). In Luke 19:11–12, a nobleman went into a far country to receive a kingdom and then returned. This nobleman went to receive the authority or right to rule over the territory that he left behind. Many times the word *kingdom* refers to the authority to rule or the exercise of that authority. When Jesus came proclaiming the kingdom of God, many might have associated it with the land of Palestine over which the son of David would establish the rule of God. Jesus uses the word *kingdom* to refer to his authority to rule, and people can enter by submitting their lives to his rule. They recognize that he has the authority to rule their lives.

The Spiritual Nature of the Kingdom. The nature of the kingdom that Jesus came to establish is present, but it is also spiritual and hidden. The spiritual nature is seen in the spiritual emphasis of Jesus' ministry. He heals a paralytic to show his power to forgive sins (Mark 2:1–12). He battles with the demons and overcomes Satan's temptations (Matt. 4:1–11). In John 18 Pilate asks Jesus whether he is the King of the Jews. Jesus avoids answering him directly, because as a Roman official Pilate would have in mind the political sense of the word *king*.[14] Jesus does make a statement about his kingdom: it is not of this world. If his kingdom were of this world, his servants would fight to keep him from being delivered over to the Jews. This definition would remove any possibility of offense against the Romans.[15] Jesus' kingdom does not have its origin in this world, and it operates with different methods. It does not advance through military activity. Pilate responds to Jesus' answer by asking, "So you are a king?" Jesus then defines his "kingly mission" in terms of truth. He has come to bear witness to the truth, and everyone who is of the truth listens to his voice (v. 37). This response summarizes his ministry of disclosing the truth about (1) his relationship to his Father in

14. Ridderbos, *John*, 593.
15. D. A. Carson, *The Gospel according to John* (Grand Rapids: Eerdmans, 1991), 594.

heaven, (2) his identity as the Christ of God, and (3) his mission to give his life as a ransom for many. His kingdom advances as people submit themselves to him as the way, the truth, and the life (14:6). Such a king would not be a threat to the Romans.

The spiritual nature of Jesus' kingdom does not mean that it is inactive in this world, or that it does not engage the world. Many of his parables define the nature of his kingdom as a mystery (Matt. 13:11; Mark 4:11; Luke 8:10).[16] George Eldon Ladd defines *mystery* as "a divine purpose, hidden in the counsels of God for long ages but finally disclosed in a new revelation of God's redemptive work."[17] This mystery refers to the way in which God's kingdom is established.[18] On one level the kingdom begins small (Matt. 13:31–32), is hidden because it works behind the scenes (v. 33), and can be rejected (vv. 8–23).[19] The Old Testament expected that when God comes to save his people to establish his kingdom, he will also destroy all their enemies.[20] The parable of the weeds shows that both the weeds and the wheat will grow together until the end of the age (vv. 24–30; see also the parable of the net in vv. 47–50). The character of Jesus' kingdom did not fit the political expectations of the people of his day, but its value is like a treasure found in the field (v. 44) or the one pearl of great price (vv. 45–46). One should sell all that one has to become a part of Jesus' kingdom.

The Future Glory of the Kingdom. Although the kingdom starts small and works behind the scenes, the end result will be great. The kingdom may start as a small seed, but it will become a

16. The Greek word is *mystērion*, translated as *secret* by the ESV, but *mystery* by the NASB and the NKJV.

17. Ladd, *Kingdom*, 52.

18. Ridderbos, *Kingdom*, 127.

19. Ladd (*Kingdom*, 56–59) explains that the parables of the mustard seed and the leaven teach that the kingdom of God is present among people in a way not previously revealed. The parable of the four soils teaches that the kingdom of God is here, but not with irresistible power.

20. Ibid., 53.

tree so that the birds of the air can make nests in it. It is like leaven, of which a small amount added to flour will permeate the whole. At the end of the age there will be a harvest during which the weeds are burned and the wheat is gathered into the barn. The parable of the weeds (and the nets) shows that after the passing of time, there will be an end to the present age (Matt. 13:30, 49).[21] A future manifestation of the kingdom is coming, when it will appear in all its glory. Jesus speaks of the end of the age and his own coming in glory in Matthew 25:31–40. There will be a separation of the sheep from the goats, and the sheep will be told to inherit the kingdom prepared for them from the foundation of the world (v. 34). A glorious manifestation of the kingdom is coming. Although it can be entered now, the full inheritance will come in the future. This kingdom will not be hidden, but will be visible to all. People from all over the world will participate in its blessings (Luke 13:29). Christ will reign not only in the hearts of his people, but also over the whole world (Rev. 11:15). This kingdom will be everlasting (Luke 1:33).[22]

Clearly, Jesus came to establish the kingdom of God. He began his ministry with a message of the kingdom (Matt. 4:17; Mark 1:15), he taught his disciples to pray "your kingdom come" (Matt. 6:10; Luke 11:2), and he exhorted them to seek first the kingdom (Matt. 6:33). It is presented as a reality that can be entered today (12:28; 21:31) and as a reality that will be established in the future (8:11; 1 Cor. 15:50). The kingdom of God has the character of an inner spiritual blessing of righteousness, peace, and joy in the Holy Spirit (Rom. 14:17), and it is an external reign that will encompass the whole world (Rev. 11:15). The parables establish that it is already present in the world but not yet in its full manifestation. The kingdom comes by the power of God, not by human wisdom or effort.

21. Ridderbos (*Kingdom*, 143) notes that a delay of judgment is emphasized in many of the parables.
22. For discussions of the kingdom, see also Geerhardus Vos, *The Kingdom of God and the Church* (Nutley, NJ: Presbyterian and Reformed, 1972).

The Suffering of the King

If the kingdom that Jesus came to establish did not match the people's expectations, it is no surprise that the kingship that Jesus came to fulfill did not match their expectations of what a king should do. Jesus did not come proclaiming that he was a king, but it is evident that he saw his ministry as being related to kingship.[23] One reason that Jesus told the demons and the people he healed to keep silent was that people might draw the wrong conclusions concerning his ministry. He began to teach his disciples what it meant for him to be king by telling them that he must go to Jerusalem to suffer, to be killed, and to rise again (Matt. 16:21–23). He even used the phrase *Son of Man* in relationship to his suffering (Mark 8:31–33; Luke 9:21–22). This phrase must have further confused the disciples, for they associated it with the glorious figure of Daniel 7. Although Jesus used the phrase in that way (Matt. 24:27; Luke 17:24), he also used it in reference to his humiliation and suffering. Peter even rebuked Jesus and said that this would never happen. The disciples did not understand how the suffering of Jesus related to his ministry. They continued discussing the glories of the kingdom and that one of them would be the greatest (Mark 9:33–34). Jesus mentioned his suffering and death to his disciples at least three times, trying to prepare them for the events that would take place in Jerusalem.

In John 10 Jesus identifies himself as the Good Shepherd. This concept opens up many associations for his work. Shepherds protect and risk their lives for the sheep (1 Sam. 17:34–35). The shepherd of Psalm 23 is identified as the Lord who provides everything that the sheep need. The kings of Israel were also considered shepherds who provided for the people. Ezekiel 34 condemns the shepherds for abandoning the sheep by not feeding them and attending to their needs. Instead, the shepherds

23. Robert Letham, *The Work of Christ* (Downers Grove, IL: InterVarsity Press, 1993), 197.

have been concerned only about meeting their own needs, and the sheep were scattered and exposed to danger. God himself pledges to shepherd the sheep and to set over the people one shepherd, his servant David, who would shepherd the people by feeding them (vv. 23–24). The description of what the shepherd needs to do to restore the sheep in verse 16 sounds much like the ministry of Jesus: seek the lost, bring back the strayed, bind up the injured, and strengthen the weak (Luke 7:22; 15:1–10). Jesus is the Shepherd King of Israel, who will provide for the needs of his sheep and will lay down his life for them.

The disciples and people of Jesus' day may not have associated the King with suffering, but Old Testament passages indicated that suffering was an aspect of the work of the coming One. The Servant of the Lord was raised up because Israel, as God's servant, had failed in her mission (Isa. 42:1–4; 49:3). The Servant's mission centers on suffering on behalf of others (52:13–53:12). Most of the language of this text focuses on sacrificial terms of innocent suffering on behalf of others—terms that are more in line with a priestly emphasis. It is possible, however, to see Davidic associations. The expression *my servant* is commonly used of royal figures (37:35). The Servant will bring justice to the ends of the earth (42:1–4), an act that is a royal responsibility. The promise of victory with the idea of dividing the spoil supports a royal emphasis.[24] These royal associations foreshadow a Suffering Servant who will also be a King.

24. Daniel I. Block, "My Servant David: Ancient Israel's Vision of the Messiah," in *Israel's Messiah in the Bible and the Dead Sea Scrolls*, ed. Richard S. Hess and M. Daniel Carroll R. (Grand Rapids: Baker, 2003), 50–51. Block emphasizes the royal Davidic role of the Messiah and tends to downplay the Messiah's other roles of Prophet and Priest, or at least sees these roles through the link with David. Thus, if Jesus was a prophetic figure, this role derived not from any link with Moses but from his connection with David. Block writes, "There is no evidence within the Old Testament itself that anyone in ancient Israel understood the office of the prophet typologically, that is, as foreshadowing 'a future figure who will play an authoritative role in the end time.'" For a different view, see chapters 2–3 of this book.

There are many ways to connect suffering with the role of Jesus as King. In the events leading up to the crucifixion, he maintained complete control of the situation. He showed his royal authority even in his humiliation. When they came to arrest him, he pronounced, "I am he," and the arresting party fell to the ground (John 18:6). He allowed himself to be arrested. He told Peter to put away the sword, and he healed the ear of a man that Peter had struck. He allowed himself to be mocked as King by the soldiers, who clothed him with a robe and put a crown of thorns on his head. Even from the cross he admitted a sinner into his kingdom and was in control of the exact moment of his death (Luke 23:43, 46). The death of the King destroyed the powers of Satan and death, delivering his people from the dominion of sin so that they could live as members of his kingdom.

It is also important that David as king experienced great suffering from his enemies. He was wrongly pursued by Saul and became a refugee, unable to live in Judah. Many of the Davidic psalms speak of his suffering at the hands of his enemies. Book 1 of the Psalter (Pss. 1–41) contains only psalms of David (a few psalms do not specify an author), and they contain more references to the wicked than any other portion of the Psalter. Psalm 1 contrasts the righteous and the wicked, and that contrast is developed in Book 1. Half the references to the wicked occur in the next thirty-nine psalms, with Psalm 37 being the most extensive discourse on the relationship between the righteous and the wicked. After the first two introductory psalms, the first Davidic psalm begins, "O LORD, how many are my foes!" (3:1). The historical title to Psalm 3 references David's fleeing from his son Absalom. David's lament psalms show the extent of his suffering and the hope of salvation that can come only from God. David had to deal with mocking (Ps. 3:2), slander and lies (4:2; 12:3–4), hatred (69:4), betrayal by friends (7:4–5), and the possibility of death (6:4). Many of his experiences foreshadow the sufferings of Christ on the cross. A few examples: not one of Christ's bones is broken (Ps. 34:20; John 19:36), he is betrayed by a close associate (Ps. 41:9; Matt. 26:23), and he is offered sour wine to drink while he is on the cross (Ps. 69:21; Matt. 27:34, 48; Mark 15:23; Luke 23:36; John 19:29).

The greatest example from the Psalms that foreshadows Jesus' suffering is Psalm 22. David describes an intense situation by using metaphors to explore the depths of his suffering (vv. 1–21).[25] His cry of being abandoned by God is the cry of Christ on the cross (Ps. 22:1; Matt. 27:46). The way in which David describes his suffering goes beyond any individual experience of suffering in the Old Testament. As Mays notes:

> There is intensity and comprehensiveness about the psalm that presses toward ultimate possibilities that lie in the event sketched in the psalm. . . . The intensity and the comprehensiveness are a fact of the psalm's composition; it is there in the text itself.[26]

The intensity and exuberance of poetic expression sets the stage for a new and expanded vision of Jesus Christ. The suffering of the individual in Psalm 22 is a type of Christ's suffering.[27] Christ experienced the shame and humiliation expressed in verses 6 through 8 as scoffers mocked him, shook their heads at him, and called on God to save him if he really trusted in God (Matt. 27:38–44; Mark 15:27–32). Some of David's metaphorical descriptions of his suffering are fulfilled literally in Christ. He was hounded by his enemies and surrounded by those who

25. No one agrees on the historical situation from which Psalm 22 originated. Calvin argues that David does not just refer to one experience of persecution but comprehends all the persecutions he experienced under Saul. John Calvin, *Psalms 1–35* (Grand Rapids: Baker, 1996), 357.

26. James L. Mays, *Psalms* (Louisville, KY: Westminster John Knox Press, 1994), 106–7.

27. For more on Psalm 22, see Belcher, *Messiah and the Psalms*, 166–72.

would do him harm (Ps. 22:16; Matt. 27:27–31; Mark 15:16–20). Crucifixion included both physical and emotional dissolution (Ps. 22:14–15, 17). His garments were divided among those who crucified him (v. 18; Matt. 27:35; Mark 15:24). The words *I thirst* (John 19:28) can be related to Psalm 22:15: "my tongue sticks to my jaws." David's suffering was real, but Christ's suffering was so much greater in being crucified and in bearing God's wrath for the sins of his people.

Just as David the king suffered in Psalm 22, Christ is mocked by the Roman soldiers with the words, "Hail, King of the Jews" (Matt. 27:29), and is crucified with the charge written on the cross, "This is Jesus, King of the Jews" (v. 37). The charge seemed so outrageous, it was a way to mock him. And yet in God's wisdom, the suffering of King Jesus was God's appointed way to save his people from their sins. Jesus rode into Jerusalem on a donkey in fulfillment of Zechariah 9:9, "Behold, your king is coming to you" (Matt. 21:5). When Pilate asked him, "Are you the King of the Jews?" he subtly answered in a way that confirmed that he was a king: "You have said so" (Matt. 27:11; Mark 15:2; Luke 23:3).[28] His and Pilate's definitions of kingship were very different from each other (John 18:36–37). Although it looked like this King was defeated in being nailed to a cross, a glorious victory was soon coming when he would divide the spoil as the fruits of his victory (Isa. 53:12).[29]

Jesus as King in Ruling at the Right Hand of the Father

The Old Testament is clear that God is King of Israel (Judg. 8:23; 1 Sam. 8:7) and of the whole earth (Pss. 22:28; 103:19; Dan.

28. The following commentaries all affirm that the statement *you have said so* is an affirmation of Jesus' kingship (Hendriksen on Matthew, Lane on Mark, Geldenhuys on Luke, and Carson on John).

29. Alec Motyer writes, "Total supremacy is, however, his by right of conquest." *The Prophecy of Isaiah: An Introduction and Commentary* (Downers Grove, IL: InterVarsity Press, 1993), 443.

4:17). If God is already King, in what sense does Jesus establish God's reign in his earthly ministry? In what way is God's sovereign rule now exercised that it was not exercised before the coming of Jesus? One answer is that the reign of God has now come into the lives of people who submit their lives to Jesus. Another answer is that in the resurrection and ascension of Jesus, he receives sovereignty in a way that he had not previously possessed it. More specifically, he received the kingdom as a human being. In Jesus' exaltation there is a reinstatement of the originally intended divine order for the earth, with a human being properly situated as God's vicegerent (someone appointed to act for another).[30]

The exaltation of Jesus begins with his resurrection, which was a momentous, life-changing, and creation-changing event. It marks his victory over sin, the power of Satan, and death. The resurrection is essential to the gospel, for if Jesus is not raised from the dead, we are still in our sins (1 Cor. 15:17–18). The gospel itself centers on the Son who was descended from David according to his human nature. Jesus was also declared to be the Son of God in power by his resurrection from the dead (Rom. 1:2–4). This declaration does not focus on his eternal status as Son; it refers to the new phase of his messianic lordship:[31] his exaltation as a human being to the position of ruler over his people, the nations, and all creation. Jesus received the kingdom as a human being, and as a human being he ascended to the right hand of his Father's throne in heaven. The incarnation did not change the Son's status as God (Phil. 2:6) but defined his human role as a Servant who had come to be obedient to the point of

---

30. Dan G. McCartney, "*Ecce Homo*: The Coming of the Kingdom as the Restoration of Human Vicegerency," *WTJ* 56, 1 (1994): 1–21. Theologians distinguish the rule of the Son as God from the rule of Christ as the God-man. The former is called the natural kingdom, and the latter is called the mediatorial kingdom. See Francis Turretin, *Institutes of Elenctic Theology*, trans. George Musgrave Giger, vol. 2 (Phillipsburg, NJ: P&R Publishing, 2014), 486; Letham, *The Work of Christ*, 197–209.

31. John Murray, *The Epistle to the Romans* (Grand Rapids: Eerdmans, 1978), 9–10.

death on the cross (vv. 7–8). Humiliation led to exaltation, and the Son received the name that is above every name and the homage of every knee as the result of his earthly ministry. In his incarnation he did not give up his deity, and in his exaltation he does not give up his humanity, but every tongue confesses that Jesus Christ is Lord. He is the image of the invisible God (Col. 1:15), who shows us what God is like, and he has come to restore the divine image in human beings through his incarnation.[32] His exalted status is shown in the description of him "as the firstborn of all creation" (v. 15). This phrase reflects Psalm 89:27, where David is called the firstborn, the highest of the kings of the earth. Christ's preeminence above all creation is evidenced in that he is before all things, that he is the Creator of all things, and that all things hold together in him (Col. 1:17).[33] As the firstborn of the dead, he takes his place as the head of the church to continue his work of reconciling all things to himself (vv. 18–20). He assumes this position not only as God, but also as man, so that now a human being has the highest and most powerful position in the universe.

Jesus now reigns above all authorities and powers as all things are put under his feet for the sake of the church (Eph. 1:20–23). He rules this universe for the good of his people and guarantees that believers, who are already seated with Christ in the heavenly places (2:6), will be with him in glory (John 17:24). The relationship of Christ's reign to humanity's exercise of dominion is brought out in Hebrews 2:5–11. Hebrews 2 quotes from Psalm 8, which in turn looks back to Genesis 1:26–28, to establish mankind's role in God's creation. The role of dominion over creation that

32. E. K. Simpson and F. F. Bruce, *Commentary on the Epistles to the Ephesians and the Colossians* (Grand Rapids: Eerdmans, 1957), 194. Bruce goes on to comment on the close association between the doctrine of man's creation in the divine image and the doctrine of the Lord's incarnation.

33. These descriptions are too lofty to refer to anything except an origin above creation.

God gave to Adam and Eve—and thus to all human beings—is fulfilled in Christ.[34] The parallels between Hebrews 2 and Psalm 8 are striking:

Psalm 8	Hebrews 2
a little lower than the heavenly beings (v. 5)	a little lower than the angels (v. 9)
crowned with glory and honor (v. 5)	crowned with glory and honor (v. 9)
put all things under his feet (v. 6)	putting everything in subjection to him (v. 8)

Just as human beings were made a little lower than the angels, so also Jesus was made a little lower than the angels. Just as human beings were crowned with glory and honor, so also Jesus was crowned with glory and honor. Just as human beings were given dominion over creation so that all things are under their feet, so the same is true for Jesus. God has left nothing outside his control, except that we do not yet see everything in subjection to him. Jesus rules this universe at the right hand of the throne of God, but not everything in creation is subject to him. A day is coming, however, when everything will be subject to him (Phil. 2:9–11; Col. 1:15–20). Psalm 8 and Genesis 1:26–28 find fulfillment in Jesus, who restores our proper place of dominion in creation. The reestablishment of God's reign in Christ also brings the restoration of our rule over creation. That one day everything will be subject to Jesus means that one day everything will be subject to us.

34. Some discuss whether the quote from Psalm 8 in Hebrews 2 refers primarily to human beings or to Christ. Kistemaker understands the reference to be first to mankind and then to Christ. Simon J. Kistemaker, *Exposition of the Epistle to the Hebrews* (Grand Rapids: Baker, 1984), 66. Hughes argues that with the phrase *a little lower than the angels*, there is a transition from man-in-general to man-in-particular (Jesus). Yet human beings are not omitted from the discussion because the destiny of mankind is fulfilled in Jesus. Philip Edgcumbe Hughes, *A Commentary on the Epistle to the Hebrews* (Grand Rapids: Eerdmans, 1977), 85–86. The ambiguity of reference makes the point that what was originally designed for human beings is fulfilled in Jesus so that the statements can apply to both. Christ, however, came to restore the dominion that was lost at the fall.

Jesus, who is fully God and fully man, will reign until all his enemies are destroyed (1 Cor. 15:24). This reign includes the conquering of people's hearts through the proclamation of the gospel and the spread of the church throughout the world. This reign will also culminate in the coming of King Jesus back to this earth, riding a white horse as he leads the armies of heaven into battle (Rev. 19:11–16). He will defeat and destroy all his enemies so that his people will also experience complete victory in the new heavens and the new earth.

Study Questions

1. How did Christ not meet the Jewish people's expectations concerning the coming King? (This issue is covered in several places in this chapter.)
2. In what ways does Christ exercise dominion during his earthly ministry?
3. Define the following characteristics of God's kingdom and state why they are important: (1) present reality of the kingdom, (2) spiritual nature of the kingdom, (3) mystery of the kingdom, and (4) future glory of the kingdom.
4. How does Jesus use the phrase *Son of Man*? How does he exercise kingly authority even in his suffering and death?
5. What new aspect of kingship came through Jesus' exaltation to the right hand of the Father?
6. How does Hebrews 2 use Psalm 8 to show Christ as fulfilling the role of dominion given to human beings?
7. If Christ is indeed King, how should we relate to him?

8

PROPHET, PRIEST, AND KING:
IMPLICATIONS FOR THE CHURCH

JESUS' FULFILLMENT of the roles of Prophet, Priest, and King has implications for the mission of the church and for the role of individual believers. The work of Jesus allows the church to fulfill its mission among the nations. When God delivered Israel out of Egypt, his purpose was to establish her as a kingdom of priests and a holy nation (Ex. 19:6). When God establishes his church and gives her the mission of proclaiming the good news of the gospel to the nations, the church also becomes "a kingdom and priests to our God" (1 Peter 2:9; Rev. 5:10). Thus, it is appropriate to reflect on how the church fulfills these roles.[1] Certain activities of the church can be described according to more than one role. For example, prayer is used in connection with both prophetic and priestly roles, so some fluidity exists in

---

1. Both Israel in the OT and the church have a witness to the nations, although that witness is carried out in different ways (see chapter 1 for a description of the mission of Israel). Continuity exists between the descriptions of Israel and the church in their roles of being a kingdom and priests (Ex. 19:5–6; 1 Peter 2:5, 9). G. K. Beale argues that Christ has installed saints in the present to function as kings and priests. See *The Book of Revelation: A Commentary on the Greek Text* (Grand Rapids: Eerdmans, 1999), 193–95.

the development of these ideas.[2] Unity in Christ's mediatorial work ensures that these roles cannot be completely separated from each other.

The church is empowered to carry out its mission by Christ's death, resurrection, and ascension. The death of Christ restores the church's broken relationship with the Father. The resurrection of Christ gives the church the power of new life to fulfill her mission. And the ascension of Christ gives confidence to the church that the mission can be accomplished. Christ sits at the right hand of the Father, directing all things for the sake of the church (Eph. 1:20–23). Christ has also equipped it to fulfill its mission by sending the Holy Spirit as his own presence to be with his people (4:11–13). The roles of prophet, priest, and king demonstrate how the church can carry out its mission as the body of Christ.

The Prophetic Ministry of the Church

Joel's Prophecy and the Day of Pentecost

On the day of Pentecost the Holy Spirit was poured out upon God's people in fulfillment of Joel 2. The book of Joel focuses on the day of the Lord, which is a day of judgment that calls for repentance from God's people (vv. 1–14). Following the judgment of the day of the Lord, there will be a full restoration. Material prosperity is promised in response to the devastation of the locust plague. The invading army will be removed (v. 20), and conditions that yield abundance will return (vv. 21–24), so that what has been destroyed will be restored (v. 25). Salvation is also promised, accompanied by great wonders in the heavens before the coming of the great and awesome day of the Lord

---

2. This chapter can only begin to offer general suggestions of how the church and individual believers carry out their prophetic, priestly, and kingly roles.

(2:28–3:3). This text is a good example of how the prophets view the future. They see the coming day of the Lord as one big event when both judgment and salvation occur together at the end of history. When God comes to save his people, he will also destroy all their enemies. Thus, Joel can lump together the outpouring of the Holy Spirit, people's calling on the name of the Lord to be saved, the wonders in the heavens, and the events on the great day of judgment. Christ did not, however, come to bring the final day of judgment. In Luke 4, when he reads from the scroll of Isaiah at the synagogue, he reads chapter 61 through the phrase "to proclaim the year of the Lord's favor" (Luke 4:19). He then rolls up the scroll and proclaims that this Scripture has been fulfilled in his audience's hearing (v. 21). The next phrase in Isaiah 61:2 is "and the day of the vengeance of our God." Instead of one big event of salvation and judgment, there are two events. Salvation is accomplished through Christ's death on the cross, and the final day of judgment is still in the future. In his first coming, Christ inaugurated his kingdom that will culminate in his second coming (see chapter 7 for a discussion of Christ's kingdom).[3]

The fulfillment of Joel's prophecy is recorded in Acts 2 on the day of Pentecost. The sending of the Holy Spirit is the culmination of Christ's work and inaugurates the messianic age, characterized by the preaching of the gospel in fulfillment of the mission that Christ gave to his disciples (Matt. 28:19–20). The aspects of Joel's prophecy that have been inaugurated relate to that mission, including the salvation of those who call on the name of the Lord and the increase in prophecy. The wonders in the heavens, described in Acts 2:19–20, will

---

3. John the Baptist had the same view as the OT prophets. He states in Matthew 3:12 that "his winnowing fork is in his hand, and he will clear his threshing floor and gather his wheat into the barn, but the chaff he will burn with unquenchable fire." Gathering the wheat is a statement of salvation, and burning the chaff is a statement of judgment.

be manifested with the great day of judgment at the second coming of Christ.[4]

The outpouring of the Spirit was essential for the church's mission to make disciples of all nations and to teach them to observe all that Christ had commanded the apostles.[5] The expectation of prophetic activity goes along with major redemptive events to explain their significance.[6] Establishing the new covenant would also generate written texts testifying to the terms of the new arrangement that God was establishing with his people.[7] Jesus promises his disciples that the Holy Spirit would be given to them to teach them all things, to bring to remembrance all that he had said to them, and to guide them into all the truth (John 14:26; 16:13). The apostles are agents of God's revelation and play a key role in laying the foundation of the church (Eph. 2:20).[8] They perform signs and wonders regularly among the people, particularly healing the sick and those afflicted with unclean spirits (Acts 5:12–16; 2 Cor. 12:12). In fulfillment of Joel 2, many others become recipients of God's revelation during the period of the apostolic church. In Acts, both major figures (Peter, Stephen, Paul) and minor figures

4. Duane A. Garrett, *Hosea, Joel* (Nashville: Broadman & Holman, 1997), 372–73. He notes that the tongues of fire are symbolic not of judgment but of the saving power of the Holy Spirit. F. F. Bruce relates the wonders in the heavens with what took place at the crucifixion, such as the sun's turning to darkness and the possibility of the full moon's appearing blood-red in the sky. He calls these unusual events tokens of the advent of the day of the Lord. *Commentary on the Book of Acts* (Grand Rapids: Eerdmans, 1977), 69.

5. Christ the Prophet continues his life-changing proclamation of the truth through the work of the Spirit, especially through regeneration and illumination. Robert Sherman, *King, Priest, and Prophet: A Trinitarian Theology of Atonement* (New York: T&T Clark, 2004), 253–55.

6. Geerhardus Vos, *Biblical Theology* (Grand Rapids: Eerdmans, 1948), 15; Michael J. Kruger, *Canon Revisited* (Wheaton, IL: Crossway, 2012), 170–74.

7. Kruger, *Canon Revisited*, 166–70.

8. Robert Letham, *The Work of Christ* (Downers Grove, IL: InterVarsity Press, 1993), 95–100. He argues that one way in which Christ continues his prophetic role is through the apostles.

(Ananias, Cornelius) see visions and dream dreams.[9] Agabus is identified as a prophet who spoke by the Holy Spirit concerning Paul's visit to Jerusalem (Acts 21:10–14). Philip had four unmarried daughters who prophesied (v. 9). The church in Corinth was gifted with those who prophesied and spoke in tongues (1 Cor. 14). This increased prophetic activity fulfilled the prophecy of Joel.

Once the apostles laid the foundation of the church, there was no need of further prophetic revelation. The focus shifted to proclaiming and explaining the Word of God that had been given to the apostles. Teaching that was not in line with apostolic teaching was accursed (Gal. 1:6–9). Anyone who added to the revelation given to the apostles was also under a curse (Rev. 22:18–19). This shift did not mean that the prophetic activity of the church ceased, but it did mean that no new revelation was given. The task of the church to preach and teach the Word of God is a continuation of the prophetic role that God has given to his people.[10]

9. David P. Moessner, "Two Lords 'at the Right Hand'? The Psalms and an Intertextual Reading of Peter's Pentecost Speech (Acts 2:14–36)," in *Literary Studies in Luke–Acts*, ed. Richard P. Thompson and Thomas E. Phillips (Macon, GA: Mercer University Press, 1998), 219. Moessner shows how Joel's statement about prophetic activity is fulfilled in the book of Acts.

10. It is beyond the scope of this book to interact with the various views concerning the continuation of prophecy. A major question centers on whether there is any difference between the apostolic church and the postapostolic church. Some, such as the New Apostolic Reformation (NAR), see little difference between the two. NAR believes that there are apostles and prophets today who function much like the apostles and prophets of the apostolic church. See R. Douglas Geivett and Holly Pivec, *A New Apostolic Reformation? A Biblical Response to a Worldwide Movement* (Wooster, OH: Weaver Book Company, 2014). Once differences between the apostolic and postapostolic church are acknowledged, the question relates to the differences between the two. For a readable, accessible approach that prophetic activity has ceased for the postapostolic church, see Samuel E. Waldron, *To Be Continued: Are Miraculous Gifts for Today?* (Merrick, NY: Calvary Press, 2005); Thomas R. Edgar, *Satisfied by the Promise of the Spirit: Affirming the Fullness of God's Provision for Spiritual Living* (Grand Rapids: Kregel, 1996). For the view that prophetic, revelatory activity continues for the church—although he argues that such prophecy is not on the same level as Scripture—see Wayne Grudem, *The*

Word and Worship

The prophetic ministry of the church is carried out in a number of ways. The corporate church fulfills a prophetic ministry by a commitment to the truth of God's Word and the faithful proclamation of the gospel. The church has been given the Word of God and, like the prophets of old, must faithfully proclaim his message. In this way the church calls people to repent of their sin and to believe in Jesus. Corporate worship, especially the singing, is a way for God's people to teach and admonish each other (Eph. 5:19; Col. 3:16) by declaring praise to God for who he is and what he has done (1 Chron. 25:3). Just as the people declared the kingship and majesty of God through song after the exodus (Ex. 15:1–21), so the church exalts the kingship of Christ by declaring his victory (Rev. 5:9).

The Prophetic Role of Elders

God helps the church fulfill this prophetic task by providing leaders who are given a prophetic role for her sake (Eph. 4:11–12).[11] Elders are charged to be faithful to the Word of God, are to be given to the ministry of prayer (Acts 6:1–6), and are to pass on the Word to others who will be faithful to it (Acts 20:28–30; 2 Tim. 2:2). God promises to accomplish his purposes and to grow the church through the preaching of the Word (Acts 2:41; 12:24; 19:20).

Gift of Prophecy in the New Testament and Today (Wheaton, IL: Crossway, 1998). For an analysis of Grudem's view, see Edmund P. Clowney, *The Church* (Downers Grove, IL: InterVarsity Press, 1995), 255–68. For the argument that the NT prophetic phenomenon is in continuity with the OT prophetic phenomenon, which leads to the conclusion that there is no need for a new kind of NT prophecy less authoritative than OT prophecy, see John W. Hilber, "Diversity of OT Prophetic Phenomenon and NT Prophecy," *WTJ* 56,2 (1994): 243–58.

11. Charles Hodge states that ministers are not prophets. It is important not to call ministers prophets because this gives the impression that ministers may receive revelation from God. It is appropriate, however, to refer to pastors as having a prophetic role in their teaching and preaching ministry. *Systematic Theology*, vol. 2 (Grand Rapids: Eerdmans, 1952), 462.

The Word establishes God's people in the truth and corrects errors of thought and behavior (2 Tim. 3:16–17). The elders must commit to regularly pray for the people of God and to faithfully preach and teach the Word of God. This commitment includes the hard work of studying (2:15), of faithfully preaching (4:1–2), and of faithfully applying the Word of God to the lives of his people to strengthen them and build them up in the faith (Eph. 4:13–14).

Implications of Prophet, Priest, and King for Preaching

The importance of the prophetic ministry of the Word of God cannot be overestimated because it is through the Word that God accomplishes his purposes (Isa. 55:10–11). Those purposes include salvation, building up God's people in the truth, protecting the church from false teaching (Jude), and hardening the hearts of people who reject the Word of God (Isa. 6:9–10; Mark 4:10–12). The church fails in her mission whenever she neglects portions of God's Word, adjusts the message of the Word to make it more acceptable to the culture, or teaches what is contrary to the Word.[12] Just as Adam and Eve in the garden and the false prophets of the Old Testament misused the word of God, so the church must guard against misusing the Word and against false prophets and teachers.

When one understands the roles of Prophet, Priest, and King and how they relate to Christ, it affects preaching and teaching. Preachers can easily develop patterns in which their preaching will flow along the same lines. One of these patterns is always ending the sermon with the obedience of Christ or his death on the cross on our behalf. Justification by faith becomes the main ending for many sermons. This commonly happens when the preacher makes the point that we are not able to fulfill whatever the text has set forth as our responsibility. We cannot do it, we

12. For reflections on how the church fulfills the prophetic, priestly, and kingly roles, see Gerry Breshears, "The Body of Christ: Prophet, Priest, or King?," *JETS* 37, 1 (March 1994): 3–26.

fall short, and so we need Christ.[13] Obviously, this is a major emphasis of Scripture, but many times such an exhortation goes against the grain of a text that might be moving in a different direction. The roles of Prophet, Priest, and King set forth the full-orbed, manifold aspects of Christ's work. A preacher can make a text relate to Christ in many ways other than his priestly work on the cross. If a text emphasizes the work of a prophet in the Old Testament, then it is appropriate to relate that text to the prophetic ministry of Christ. Many of the texts of wisdom literature can be related to the teaching ministry of Jesus, or to an aspect of Jesus as the wisdom of God.[14] If a text is encouraging the people of God to be obedient to him, the continuing work of Christ's priestly ministry after his ascension can encourage us to be obedient through the power of the Spirit, to help us in our sanctification. If a text emphasizes the struggle with sin and victory over sin, Christ as King—who has won our victory over sin and has empowered us to live for him—can be emphasized. By understanding the different aspects of Christ's ministry based on his roles as Prophet, Priest, and King, the preacher is better able to preach all aspects of the Christian life, including justification, sanctification, and glorification.

The Prophetic Role of Individual Believers

The prophetic role is also important for individual believers. The Heidelberg Catechism connects the prophetic, priestly, and

13. Some of the grace-based approaches and the redemptive-history-only approaches fall into this pattern of consistently ending with justification by faith. For further analysis of the different redemptive-history approaches, see Robert J. Cara, "Redemptive-Historical Themes in the *Westminster Larger Catechism*," in *The Westminster Confession of Faith in the 21st Century*, ed. Ligon Duncan, 3 vols. (Ross-shire, UK: Christian Focus, 2009), 3:55–76. For an analysis of the problems of a truncated view of sanctification, see David Powlison, "How Does Sanctification Work? (Part 1)," *Journal of Biblical Counseling* (March 2013): 49–66. For a historical analysis of these issues with modern-day implications, see Mark Jones, *Antinomianism* (Phillipsburg, NJ: P&R Publishing, 2013).

14. Daniel J. Ebert IV, *Wisdom Christology* (Phillipsburg, NJ: P&R Publishing, 2011).

kingly roles to the believer's life through how Christ fulfills those roles (see also WCF 8.1; WLC 41–45; WSC 23–26). Question 31 reads, "Why is he called Christ, meaning, 'anointed'?" The answer is given in terms of how he is Prophet, Priest, and King. Jesus is described "as our chief prophet and teacher who perfectly reveals to us the secret counsel and will of God concerning our deliverance." Then Question 32 asks, "But why are you called a Christian?" The answer: "Because by faith I am a member of Christ (1 Cor. 12:12–27) and so I share in his anointing (Acts 2:17; 1 John 2:27). I am anointed to confess his name" (Matt. 10:32; Rom. 10:9–10; Heb. 13:15).[15] The anointing of the Holy Spirit is mentioned in 1 John 2:27 in the context of dealing with false teachers who deny that Jesus is the Christ. This anointing refers to the ministry of the Holy Spirit in bringing people to an understanding of the gospel and of the person of Christ. The Spirit regenerates and indwells believers and continues his ministry of illuminating their minds to the truth of God's Word. This anointing is a remedy against false teaching because the believers that John is writing to are not inferior to the false teachers. They also have the Spirit who teaches them. John is not denying the importance of teachers in the church when he says that the believers have no need for anyone to teach them. Rather, he is invalidating the authority of the false teachers.[16] He also needs to encourage the believers to continue under difficult circumstances, following what they know to be true.[17]

The prophetic role of believers consists in the faithful handling of the Word of God and its use in their daily lives. Every believer has a prophetic role in fulfillment of God's promise

15. The Heidelberg Catechism (Grand Rapids: Board of Education of the Christian Reformed Church in America, 1975), adopted by the United Reformed Churches in North America.
16. Gary M. Burge, *Letters of John* (Grand Rapids: Zondervan, 1996), 132.
17. George L. Parsenios, *First, Second, and Third John* (Grand Rapids: Baker, 2014), 90.

(Acts 2).[18] There are many ways to think of this role. A believer must be committed to study and understand the Word of God to fight against sin in his or her own life (Heb. 4:12–13), to minister to others, and to speak the truth in love (Eph. 4:15).[19] A father must understand Scripture to lead his family in the study and use of God's Word, and a mother must be able to apply the Word of God to her children daily.[20] In this way the Bible becomes foundational to everything a believer does in life. Even when Christ comes again, the prophetic role will not come to an end, but the original prophetic purpose that God had for Adam will be fulfilled. In the new heavens and the new earth, we will correctly handle the Word of God and speak only the truth about God and the world.[21]

The Priestly Ministry of the Church

The "Service" of the Levites

The corporate church fulfills its priestly role as the body of Christ in several ways.[22] The worship of the church is service to

18. Vern S. Poythress, "Modern Spiritual Gifts as Analogous to Apostolic Gifts: Affirming Extraordinary Works of the Spirit within Cessationist Theology," *JETS* 39, 1 (1996): 71–101. He gives a biblical framework for thinking about gifts of the Spirit as analogous and subordinate to the ministry of Christ. Poythress has a chart that shows how the prophetic, kingly, and priestly roles (1) originate in Christ, (2) are continued in the works of the apostles, who have a unique divine authority, and (3) are then carried out by elders and pastors (in a special office) and by every believer (in a general sense). The latter two categories are under the biblical authority of Christ and the apostles.

19. Karl H. Hertz defines the role of the Christian as prophet, priest, and king, but he distorts the prophetic role of believers by not defining it according to Scripture and by limiting the discussion to speaking the truth to social injustice. *Everyman a Priest* (Philadelphia: Muhlenberg Press, 1960).

20. Gene Edward Veith Jr. and Mary J. Moerbe, *Family Vocation: God's Calling in Marriage, Parenting, and Childhood* (Wheaton, IL: Crossway, 2012). This book specifically discusses the vocations of parenthood under the office of father and the office of mother.

21. Wayne Grudem, *Systematic Theology* (Grand Rapids: Zondervan, 1994), 630.

22. For the complex nature of how the term *body of Christ* is used in the NT, see Paul S. Minear, *Images of the Church in the New Testament* (Louisville, KY: Westminster

the Lord, both to its members and to the world. This aspect of service continues an Old Testament emphasis on the work of the priests and Levites. The ministry of the Levites at the tabernacle is called their "service" (Num. 7:5, 7, 8; 8:22).[23] Later, some of the Levites are put in charge of "the service of song in the house of the LORD" (1 Chron. 6:31). Once the ark came to rest in Jerusalem, their job shifted from carrying the tabernacle to assisting the sons of Aaron in the service at the house of the Lord. Their tasks included (1) helping with the showbread, the flour of the grain offering, the wafers of the unleavened bread, the baked offering, and the offering mixed with oil, and (2) praising the Lord every morning and evening when the burnt offerings were presented (23:26–32). The work of the priests is also called their "work of service" (1 Chron. 24:3; 2 Chron. 8:14; Luke 1:23). This included keeping the Passover and sacrificing burnt offerings (2 Chron. 35:16). The word *service* is also used of the ministry that Christ has received in mediating a better covenant (Heb. 8:6). He is a minister (*leitourgos*) in the heavenly temple (v. 2). Hebrews 10:11 uses the verb form of *leitourgos* for the priest who stands daily at his service by offering sacrifices. The same verb can also be used of Christian worship (Acts 13:2).[24]

The Priestly Ministry of Elders in Worship

The service of worship carried out by the priests and the Levites at the Old Testament temple is now carried out by

---

John Knox Press, 2004). The aspect of the body of Christ relevant to this discussion is this: "His headship means that his body continues the work of reconciliation (ch. 1:19), continues its participation in his sufferings (chs. 1:24; 3:5f.), continues his ministry of love (ch. 3:14) as a sign to the world of Christ's victory over its gods" (207). The references are to the book of Colossians.

23. The Hebrew word *avodah* (עבדה) is translated *leitourgia* by the Greek OT. The verb form is *leioturgeō*.

24. For an analysis of this word group, see T. F. Torrance, *Royal Priesthood: A Theology of Ordained Ministry*, 2nd ed. (Edinburgh: T&T Clark, 1993), 15–20. Torrance shows that the word group *leitourgia* is used of the ministry of the church in the NT.

Christ in the heavenly temple and by Christians in the spiritual temple of God's new covenant people.[25] Although Jesus is the only High Priest through whom we approach God, the elders have an important priestly role in assisting the church in worshiping God.[26] They oversee the worship service, and they lead God's people in worship. Thus they guard the spiritual temple of God by making sure that worship is God-honoring. The elders call God's people to worship and lead them in its various prayers.[27] Like the priests of the Old Testament, they lead God's people in confession of sin and pronounce over them God's benediction.[28] It is appropriate to see pastoral work as a vocation in which one is supported by the church in the work of ministry (1 Cor. 9:10–11; 1 Tim. 5:17). Pastors and elders must also make themselves available for pastoral care when

25. Paul finds the community of the church, particularly the church composed of Jew and Gentile, and the church's spiritual activities prefigured in the OT. Even the work of priests and Levites is given to Gentiles in a future age (Isa. 66:18–21). Some have called this aspect of Paul's hermeneutic "ecclesiocentric." See Richard B. Hays, *Echoes of Scripture in the Letters of Paul* (New Haven, CT: Yale University Press, 1989), xiii, 84–86. An emphasis on the church as prefigured in the OT does not have to be in competition or in contrast with an emphasis on Christ as also prefigured in the OT.

26. Jack Dennis Kinneer, "Priesthood and Ministry," in *Order in the Offices: Essays Defining the Roles of Church Officers*, ed. Mark R. Brown (Duncansville, PA: Classic Presbyterian Government Resources, 1993), 180–201; see also the chapter by Charles Dennison, "Worship and Office," 257–79. Ryan M. McGraw makes the important distinction that ministers are not priests who present people holy in the sight of God, but that their role is to present Christ to people and he makes them holy. "The Benediction in Corporate Worship," *The Confessional Presbyterian* 7 (2011): 119.

27. For an analysis of the different public prayers in worship and their function in the worship service, see Andrew Blackwood, *Leading in Public Prayer* (Grand Rapids: Baker, 1957); Hughes Oliphant Old, *Leading in Prayer: A Workbook for Worship* (Grand Rapids: Eerdmans, 1995).

28. For a detailed analysis of how benedictions functioned in the OT, the justification for the continuing use of benedictions in the NT church, and the proper use of benedictions in a worship service, see McGraw, "The Benediction," 111–22. He connects the continuing use of benedictions to the ministry of the Word carried out by priests in the OT, rather than to their specific role as priests. But as long as ministers are not called priests, there is not a problem connecting the benediction to a priestly role of the minister of the Word.

members of the congregation need spiritual help and counsel (1 Peter 5:1–2).[29]

The Priestly Role of Individual Believers

Individual believers also actively participate in worship by responding to God's Word and by singing. The service of song has a prophetic function (Col. 3:16–17), but it also has a priestly aspect. The church is a holy house, a spiritual priesthood, offering spiritual sacrifices acceptable to God through Jesus Christ (1 Peter 2:5).[30] In the Old Testament, the fellowship offering—also called the peace offering (Lev. 3)—could be brought for a variety of reasons: thanksgiving; a vow offering; or a freewill offering (6:11–18) in response to God's goodness in the life of the worshiper. The church in worship continues to offer "a sacrifice of praise" to acknowledge God's name (Heb. 13:15). Through their formal worship they serve God, other believers, and unbelievers, giving testimony to God and calling people to acknowledge him.[31]

Individual believers also have a priestly role to fulfill in their daily lives (normally called *the priesthood of believers*). Again, Heidelberg Catechism Question 31 asks, "Why is he called Christ, meaning, 'anointed'?" The answer related to the office of a priest says that Christ is "our only high priest who has set us free by

29. Hodge (*Systematic Theology*, 2:467) denies that ministers carry out a priestly function and affirms that they are priests only in the sense in which all believers are priests: they have liberty of access to God through Christ. Letham (*The Work of Christ*, 122) limits the priesthood to the corporate church and not to individual believers, partly because individual believers do not represent anybody. A more satisfying view is given by Albert Vanhoye, *Old Testament Priests and the New Priest* (Petersham, MA: St. Bede's Publications, 1986), 312–18. He argues that there is only one priest in the full sense of the term (Christ) and that Christians possess a common priesthood through his mediation, which brings about a participation (on a different level) in his priesthood.

30. Edward G. Selwyn, *The First Epistle of Peter* (London: Macmillan, 1946), 292. He draws parallels between (1) the work of the Levites and priests and (2) the Christian life of the members of the church.

31. Grudem (*Systematic Theology*, 630) argues that Christians will be priests forever by offering eternal worship to the Lamb before the throne of God (Rev. 22:3–4).

the one sacrifice of his body, and who continually pleads our cause with the Father." Then Question 32 asks, "Why are you called a Christian?" The answer related to our priestly role is "to present myself to him as a living sacrifice of thanks (Rom. 12:1; 1 Peter 2:5, 9)." The sacrifice of praise that a Christian offers is a continual sacrifice (Heb. 13:15), not limited to the formal worship of the church. A believer is always to be giving thanks and praise to God. In fact, our lives are to demonstrate a willingness to give up everything for the sake of Jesus Christ. We are to deny ourselves, daily take up our cross, and follow him. We are to live in constant self-denial so that our lives become a sacrifice for Christ. We are to present our bodies as living sacrifices to God, not being conformed to this world but by being transformed by the renewal of our minds (Rom. 12:1–2). Not just our minds but our bodies are to be devoted to pleasing God. Our bodies are temples of the Holy Spirit who lives in us, so we should flee sexual immorality (1 Cor. 6:19–20). Just as holiness was a major focus of the priests in the Old Testament, so believers are set apart to live holy lives for God.

Christians carry out their priestly role in a number of ways. The mission of the church includes taking the gospel to all nations. Paul understands his ministry of taking the gospel to the Gentiles to be "in the priestly service of the gospel" so that the offering of the Gentiles might be acceptable to God (Rom. 15:16). Paul also describes his life as a drink offering being poured out in fulfillment of his ministry (2 Tim. 4:6) and says that he bears on his body the "marks of Jesus" (Gal. 6:17). These marks (*stigmata*) of Jesus are scars of the persecution and physical suffering that Paul has received in his apostolic ministry.[32] Jesus received these marks by his death on the cross when he offered himself as a sacrifice for sin. The persecution—and even death—that believers experience for the sake of Christ can be related to

32. Timothy George, *Galatians* (Nashville: Broadman & Holman, 1994), 441–42.

the priestly role of living for Christ and taking the gospel to the nations. Persecuted Christians offer their lives as sacrifices in a special way, serving the world by faithfully giving testimony to the truth of Christ.[33]

Christians are to serve in other ways as part of offering their lives as sacrifices to God. The sacrifice of praise in Hebrews 13:15 is to be offered continually. Such spiritual sacrifices, which are pleasing to God, include doing good and sharing with others (v. 16).[34] Intercessory prayer and confession of sin are related to suffering, sickness, and healing (James 5:13–16).[35] The elders play a role in this ministry, as they are specifically mentioned in James 5:14, but individual Christians can also minister by interceding for the needs of others. The physical needs of the widows in Acts 6 are so important that the church sets aside deacons to be sure that these needs are met. The church's primary responsibility is to care for her own, without neglecting "the unique dispensation of service given to every born-again believer through the providential ordering of God"[36] (see Gal. 6:10). Individual Christians are sent into the world to do the good works that God has prepared beforehand that they should do.

33. In Colossians 1:24 Paul states, "Now I rejoice in my sufferings for your sake, and in my flesh I am filling up what is lacking in Christ's afflictions for the sake of his body, that is, the church." The focus of this verse is not the complete satisfaction that Christ has made to his Father by his death, but the relationship of the members of Christ's body with his sufferings. Calvin writes, "Christ has suffered *once* in his own person, so he suffers *daily* in his members and in this way there are *filled up* those sufferings which the Father hath appointed for his body by his decree." "Philippians," in *Calvin's Commentaries* (Grand Rapids: Baker, 1996), 21:164.

34. Philip E. Hughes identifies these spiritual sacrifices as praise to God and compassionate service to others. *A Commentary on the Epistle to the Hebrews* (Grand Rapids: Eerdmans, 1977), 583.

35. David P. Nystrom, *James* (Grand Rapids: Zondervan, 1997), 303. He notes that the theme of this passage is prayer because it is mentioned in every verse: the prayer of the individual (James 5:13), the prayer of the elders (vv. 14–15), the prayer of friends and companions for one another (v. 16), and the prayer of the righteous prophet Elijah (vv. 17–18).

36. George, *Galatians*, 427.

The priestly ministry also includes ministering to one's own family. The priests in the Old Testament had a teaching role related to the law of God and the worship of God. Parents also serve a priestly role for their children by bringing them to worship, by presenting them to the church for baptism, by teaching them the truths of the faith, and by being a conduit of blessing to them.[37]

One way that believers can serve both their family and others is through work. Adam's work in the garden was related to the priestly role because the two verbs used of Adam's work (Gen. 2:15) were later used of the work of the Levites at the tabernacle (see chapter 1). Work is not just an occupation or a way to make money; it is a *vocation*, which means a calling from God. Before the Reformation only the priests were considered to have a vocation, and this applied only to their spiritual work. The Reformation extended *vocation* to include the work of everyone, so that a banker, a janitor, or a homemaker could be seen as having a vocation from God.[38] Whatever work God has given a believer to do is his or her calling for that particular time in that person's life. This transforms work because if it is a vocation from God, it should be done to the glory of God in the service of others. God uses this work to supply the needs of others. Every Christian should view a daily job as a way to minister to his or her family by providing for their needs and as a way to serve others. Thus everyday, ordinary life is transformed by the presence of God.[39]

37. Veith and Moerbe, *Family Vocation*, has sections on the vocations of parenthood and childhood.

38. For a discussion of work as vocation and the significance of the Reformation in the historical development of this idea, see Gene Edward Veith Jr., *God at Work: Your Christian Vocation in All of Life* (Wheaton, IL: Crossway, 2002).

39. For an insightful analysis of the problems of work (idolatry and idleness) and how the gospel impacts work, see Sebastian Traeger and Greg Gilbert, *The Gospel at Work: How Working for King Jesus Gives Purpose and Meaning to Our Jobs* (Grand Rapids: Zondervan, 2013).

The Kingly Ministry of the Church

The Rule of Elders

The church fulfills a kingly role by participating in the victory and reign of Christ.[40] The proclamation of his reign is essential to the mission of the church and gives others the opportunity to submit their lives to King Jesus. The church also engages in spiritual warfare by using the spiritual weapons that God has given her to battle spiritual forces in heavenly places (Eph. 6:10–20). Thus she participates in defeating Satan through the power of Christ and has the promise that Satan will be crushed under her feet (Rom. 16:20). Elders assist the church in this kingly role by their authority to govern. Christ is the head of the church and rules the world for the sake of his people (Eph. 1:22). Elders govern the church under the authority of Christ (1 Peter 5:1–2). The term *elder* has a rich Old Testament heritage that refers to someone with wisdom and maturity.[41] Elders are also called *pastors* (Acts 20:28), the term for *shepherds* that expresses care for the spiritual health of the flock.[42] Elders are also designated as *overseers* (v. 28), a term that emphasizes the activities of leading, guiding, and ruling.[43] The oversight of the church includes the authority to admit someone into the membership of the church (Matt. 16:19), the protection of the flock from false teachers (Acts

40. For a discussion of the source of church power (Christ), the rule or law of church power (the Word of God), and the spiritual nature of church power, see James Bannerman, *The Church of Christ*, 2 vols. (Edinburgh: Banner of Truth Trust, 1974), 1:187–222, 223–34; Guy Waters, *How Jesus Runs the Church* (Phillipsburg, NJ: P&R Publishing, 2011), 64–80.

41. Alexander Strauch, *Biblical Eldership*, rev. ed. (Littleton, CO: Lewis and Roth, 1995), 122–23.

42. It is significant that kings in the OT were considered shepherds. It was the failure of Israel's shepherds that led to the judgment of exile (Ezek. 34).

43. John R. Sittema, *With a Shepherd's Heart: Reclaiming the Pastoral Office of Elder* (Grandville, MI: Reformed Fellowship, 1996), 6. See also Cornelius Van Dam, *The Elder: Today's Ministry Rooted in All of Scripture* (Phillipsburg, NJ: P&R Publishing, 2009).

20:29), and the exercise of church discipline (Matt. 18:15–18; 1 Cor. 5:9–12).⁴⁴ Church discipline sounds harsh to many people, but it has several goals that benefit both the church and the individual under discipline. Goals of church discipline include restoring the sinner, protecting the innocent, maintaining the purity of the church as separated from the world, and acting as a warning to others in the church.⁴⁵

The Dominion of Individual Believers

Individual believers also participate in a kingly role by being members of Christ's kingdom and being subject to Christ the King.⁴⁶ Heidelberg Catechism Question 31 asks, "Why is he called Christ, meaning, 'anointed'?" The answer related to the office of a king says that Christ is "our eternal king who governs us by his word and Spirit, and who guards us and keeps us in the freedom he has won for us (Matt. 28:18–20; John 10:28; Rev. 12:10–11)." Then Question 32 asks, "Why are you called a Christian?" The answer related to our kingly role is "to strive with a good conscience against sin and the devil in this life (Gal. 5:16–17; Eph. 5:11; 1 Tim. 1:18–19), and afterward to reign with Christ over all creation for all eternity (Matt. 25:34; 2 Tim. 2:12)." Part of Christ's work was to restore to human beings the exalted place in God's creation that they are supposed to occupy (Gen. 1:26–28; Ps. 8; Heb. 2:5–9). Believers are to rule over God's creation, exercising

44. For practical help in church discipline, see Jay Adams, *Handbook of Church Discipline* (Grand Rapids: Zondervan, 1986); and for practical help in dealing with conflict in the church, see Ken Sande, *The Peacemaker*, 3rd ed. (Grand Rapids: Baker, 2004).

45. Michael Dixon, *What Is Church Discipline?* (Phillipsburg, NJ: P&R Publishing, forthcoming).

46. For a discussion of the relationship between the kingdom and the church, see Geerhardus Vos, *The Kingdom of God and the Church* (Nutley, NJ: Presbyterian and Reformed, 1972), 77–90. He argues that the church is part of the kingdom of God, but that the kingdom of God is broader than the church. Every legitimate province of human life can become a part of God's kingdom because of the absolute supremacy of God in all things.

dominion over it as his stewards (Gen. 1:26–28).[47] This dominion includes mastery over different areas of creation. Proverbs 25:2 states, "It is the glory of God to conceal things, but the glory of kings is to search things out." The use of *Elohim* for *God* and the reference to the heavens and the earth in the proverb pair of verse 3 suggest that what God conceals includes his wisdom in his acts of creation.[48]

In contrast, the glory of kings is to search things out, an activity that should not be limited to judicial decisions or affairs of state.[49] Kings can investigate God's creation (1) to understand how it works, (2) to assist others in that understanding by naming and explaining it, and (3) by constructing things to show its beauties.[50] Both Adam (Gen. 2:19) and Solomon (1 Kings 4:33) searched things out to discover how the world works. People continue this activity today in numerous ways, from a company that develops a better formula to clean certain types of floors to scientists who explore how creation works.[51] Dominion also includes using creation for the benefit of others and caring for it. We labor under Christ's authority and do all our work for his glory (1 Cor. 10:31). As individuals, we also put on the full armor of God so that we can stand against the wiles of the devil (Eph. 6:11). We seek to extend the reign of Christ by standing for the

47. Greg Forster, *Joy for the World* (Wheaton, IL: Crossway, 2014), 166. He defines stewardship in a broad way to include all of life, not just stewardship of the environment. In Part 2 he defines the role of Christians in terms of prophet, priest, and king.

48. Bruce K. Waltke, *The Book of Proverbs: Chapters 15–31* (Grand Rapids: Eerdmans, 2005), 311.

49. Derek Kidner, *Proverbs* (Downers Grove, IL: InterVarsity Press, 1964), 157. He limits the search when he sees this verse as primarily praising administrative probes into events in the kingdom, and he omits academic research.

50. Even pagan kings unknowingly demonstrate this truth by their building projects, such as the pyramids in Egypt and the hanging gardens in Babylon, which are each considered one of the seven wonders of the ancient world.

51. For the evidence that the flowering of science took place in the sixteenth century within the theological assumptions unique to Christianity, see R. Hooykaas, *Religion and the Rise of Modern Science* (Grand Rapids: Eerdmans, 1972); Rodney Stark, *For the Glory of God* (Princeton, NJ: Princeton University Press, 2003).

truth of his Word and by protecting and defending what he has entrusted to our care. This rule includes almost anything over which we have oversight and control, but it especially includes parents' protecting and defending their children from the harmful influences of the world. All our actions and our use of resources should advance the kingdom of Christ. When Christ comes, we will reign with him forever in the new heavens and the new earth (Rev. 22:5).

Conclusion

The examination of the roles of prophet, priest, and king began in the early chapters of Genesis with Adam and Eve in the garden of Eden, where God established the proper place of mankind within his creation. The garden was a special place of his presence, where Adam and Eve had communion with him. God gave to the pinnacle of his creation the kingly role of ruling under his authority. He also gave to Adam work in the garden, work that is described with two verbs later used for the priestly work of the Levites. He also gave to Adam his word, which Adam passed on to Eve and which became the center of their discussion with Satan. Adam and Eve failed in their prophetic role by mishandling the word. They failed in their kingly role by not exercising dominion over the serpent, and they failed in their priestly role by not protecting the sacred space of the garden through casting out the serpent. Disobedience led to expulsion from the garden and a struggle to carry out their God-given roles.

The prophetic, priestly, and kingly roles needed to be redefined so that it would be clear how human beings were to fulfill them. All three roles are exemplified in Abraham and then are defined in the nation of Israel's offices of prophet, priest, and king. Christ fulfills and transforms these roles in his earthly ministry and continues to exercise them in his heavenly ministry from the right hand of the Father. The corporate church, the elders of the church, and individual believers continue to carry out these roles. It is helpful to distinguish these roles from one another to define them, but in reality it is difficult to completely separate them. Many activities of Christians can be defined by these roles. This chapter closes with an exercise that should help believers think about how these roles can be lived out in their lives.

Worksheet on the Implications of the Prophetic, Priestly, and Kingly Roles for Believers

1. Work: How can God use my work to bring honor to himself?
   (a) How can God use me in my work to spread the truth of God's Word (prophetic role)?
   (b) How can God use me in my work to serve others (priestly role)?
   (c) How can God use me in my work to rule over those areas for which he has given me responsibility, to be a good steward of what has been entrusted to me, and to extend his rule and kingdom in this world (kingly role)?
2. Family roles: The following questions can be applied to husbands and fathers, wives and mothers, and also children. Supply the family role that best fits your situation.
   (a) How can your role as a family member spread the truth of God's Word?
   (b) How can your role as a family member serve your family?
   (c) How can your role as a family member honor God by properly interacting with other family members, by being good stewards with what God has entrusted you, and by extending God's rule and kingdom?
3. Prayer: How does prayer relate to these roles?
   (a) How can God use prayer (or my prayers) to spread the truth of his Word?

    (b) How can God use prayer (or my prayers) to serve others?

    (c) How can God use prayer (or my prayers) to extend his rule and kingdom in this world?

4. The role of elders: How does the role of elder fulfill these roles?

    (a) How do elders carry out a prophetic role in the ministry of the church?

    (b) What implications are there for preaching and teaching when one understands the roles of prophet, priest, and king?

    (c) How do elders carry out a priestly role in their ministry in the church?

    (d) How do elders carry out a kingly role in their function in the church?

5. Worship/singing (the following passages can be used to answer these questions: Exodus 15, 1 Chronicles 25:3, Ephesians 5:19, Colossians 3:16, and Revelation 5:9):

    (a) How can God use worship/singing in a prophetic way?

    (b) How can God use worship/singing to minister to others?

    (c) How can God use worship/singing to express his kingship?

Selected Bibliography

Amerding, Carl. "Were David's Sons Really Priests?" In *Current Issues in Biblical and Patristic Interpretation*, edited by Gerald F. Hawthorne, 75–86. Grand Rapids: Eerdmans, 1975.

Bannerman, James. *The Church of Christ*. 2 vols. Edinburgh: Banner of Truth Trust, 1974.

Bateman, Herbert W., IV., Darrell L. Bock, and Gordon H. Johnston. *Jesus the Messiah*. Grand Rapids: Kregel, 2012.

Bavinck, Herman. *Reformed Dogmatics*. Vol. 3, *Sin and Salvation in Christ*. Grand Rapids: Baker, 2006.

Beale, G. K. *The Temple and the Church's Mission: A Biblical Theology of the Dwelling Place of God*. Downers Grove, IL: InterVarsity Press, 2004.

Belcher, Richard P., Jr. *The Messiah and the Psalms*. Ross-shire, UK: Christian Focus, 2006.

Berkhof, Louis. *Systematic Theology*. Grand Rapids: Eerdmans, 1941.

Borland, James A. *Christ in the Old Testament: Old Testament Appearances of Christ in Human Form*. Ross-shire, UK: Christian Focus, 1999.

Breshears, Gerry. "The Body of Christ: Prophet, Priest, or King?" *JETS* 37, 1 (March 1994): 3–26.

Cara, Robert J. "Redemptive-Historical Themes in the *Westminster Larger Catechism*." In *The Westminster Confession of Faith in the 21st Century*, edited by Ligon Duncan, 3:55–76. 3 vols. Ross-shire, UK: Christian Focus, 2009.

Clowney, Edmund P. *The Church*. Downers Grove, IL: InterVarsity Press, 1995.

———. "The Final Temple." *WTJ* 35, 2 (1972): 156–89.

Crump, David. *Jesus the Intercessor: Prayer and Christology in Luke–Acts*. Grand Rapids: Baker, 1992.

Davies, John A. "Discerning between Good and Evil: Solomon as a New Adam in 1 Kings." *WTJ* 73, 1 (2011): 39–57.

Day, John, ed. *King and Messiah in Israel and the Ancient Near East.* Sheffield, UK: Sheffield Academic Press, 1998.

Deenick, Karl. "Priest and King or Priest-King in 1 Samuel 2:35." *WTJ* 73, 2 (2011): 325–39.

Dennison, Charles. "Worship and Office." In *Order in the Offices: Essays Defining the Roles of Church Officers,* edited by Mark R. Brown, 257–79. Duncansville, PA: Classic Presbyterian Government Resources, 1993.

de Vaux, Roland. *Ancient Israel: Its Life and Institutions.* Grand Rapids: Eerdmans, 1961.

Dutcher-Walls, Patricia. "The Circumspection of the King: Deuteronomy 17:16–17 in Its Ancient Social Context." *JBL* 121 (2002): 603–4.

Ebert, Daniel J., IV. *Wisdom Christology.* Phillipsburg, NJ: P&R Publishing, 2011.

Edgar, Thomas R. *Satisfied by the Promise of the Spirit: Affirming the Fullness of God's Provision for Spiritual Living.* Grand Rapids: Kregel, 1996.

Frame, John M. *Systematic Theology: An Introduction to Christian Belief.* Phillipsburg, NJ: P&R Publishing, 2013.

Geivett, R. Douglas, and Holly Pivec. *A New Apostolic Reformation? A Biblical Response to a Worldwide Movement.* Wooster, OH: Weaver Book Company, 2014.

Gordon, Robert P., ed. *The Place Is Too Small for Us.* Winona Lake, IN: Eisenbrauns, 1995.

Grudem, Wayne. *The Gift of Prophecy in the New Testament and Today.* Wheaton, IL: Crossway, 1998.

———. *Systematic Theology.* Grand Rapids: Zondervan, 1994.

Haran, Menahem. *Temples and Temple-Service in Ancient Israel.* Winona Lake, IN: Eisenbrauns, 1985.

Harris, R. Laird, Gleason L. Archer, Jr., and Bruce K. Waltke, eds. *Theological Wordbook of the Old Testament.* 2 vols. Chicago: Moody Press, 1980.

Hengstenberg, E. W. *Christology of the Old Testament.* Grand Rapids: Kregel, 1970.

Hess, Richard S., and M. Daniel Carroll R., eds. *Israel's Messiah in the Bible and the Dead Sea Scrolls*. Grand Rapids: Baker, 2003.

Hilber, John W. "Diversity of OT Prophetic Phenomenon and NT Prophecy." *WTJ* 56, 2 (1994): 243–58.

Hoeksema, Herman. *Reformed Dogmatics*. 2nd ed. Grandville, MI: Reformed Free Publishing Association, 2004.

Hooykaas, R. *Religion and the Rise of Modern Science*. Grand Rapids: Eerdmans, 1972.

Horton, Michael. *The Christian Faith*. Grand Rapids: Zondervan, 2011.

Huffmon, Herbert B. "The Covenant Lawsuit in the Prophets." *JBL* 78 (1959): 286–95.

Jeon, Yong Ho. "The Retroactive Re-evaluation Technique with Pharaoh's Daughter and the Nature of Solomon's Corruption in 1 Kings 1–12." *TynBul* 62, 1 (2011): 15–40.

Jones, Mark. *Antinomianism*. Phillipsburg, NJ: P&R Publishing, 2013.

Kinneer, Jack Dennis. "Priesthood and Ministry." In *Order in the Offices: Essays Defining the Roles of Church Officers*, edited by Mark R. Brown, 180–201. Duncansville, PA: Classic Presbyterian Government Resources, 1993.

Kruger, Michael J. *Canon Revisited*. Wheaton, IL: Crossway, 2012.

Ladd, George Eldon. *The Gospel of the Kingdom*. Grand Rapids: Eerdmans, 1959.

Letham, Robert. *The Work of Christ*. Downers Grove, IL: InterVarsity Press, 1993.

Limburg, James. "The Root ריב and the Prophetic Lawsuit Speeches." *JBL* 88 (1969): 291–304.

Lioy, Dan. *Axis of Glory: A Biblical and Theological Analysis of the Temple Motif in Scripture*. New York: Lang, 2010.

Longman, Tremper, III. *Immanuel in Our Place*. Phillipsburg, NJ: P&R Publishing, 2001.

McCartney, Dan G. "*Ecce Homo*: The Coming of the Kingdom as the Restoration of Human Vicegerency." *WTJ* 56, 1 (1994): 1–21.

McGraw, Ryan M. "The Benediction in Corporate Worship." *The Confessional Presbyterian* 7 (2011): 111–22.

Merrill, Eugene. "Royal Priesthood: An Old Testament Messianic Motif." *BSac* 150 (January–March 1993): 50–61.

Miller, Patrick. *The Religion of Ancient Israel*. Louisville, KY: Westminster John Knox Press, 2000.

Minear, Paul S. *Images of the Church in the New Testament*. Louisville, KY: Westminster John Knox Press, 2004.

Moessner, David P. "Two Lords 'at the Right Hand'? The Psalms and an Intertextual Reading of Peter's Pentecost Speech (Acts 2:14–36)." In *Literary Studies in Luke–Acts*, edited by Richard P. Thompson and Thomas E. Phillips, 215–32. Macon, GA: Mercer University Press, 1998.

Owen, John. *The Priesthood of Christ: Its Necessity and Nature*. Ross-shire, UK: Christian Focus, 2010.

Paul, M. J. "The Order of Melchizedek (Ps 110:4 and Heb 7:3)." *WTJ* 49, 1 (1987): 195–211.

Powlison, David. "How Does Sanctification Work? (Part 1)." *Journal of Biblical Counseling* (March 2013): 49–66.

Poythress, Vern S. "Modern Spiritual Gifts as Analogous to Apostolic Gifts: Affirming Extraordinary Works of the Spirit within Cessationist Theology." *JETS* 39, 1 (1996): 71–101.

———. *The Shadow of Christ in the Law of Moses*. Phillipsburg, NJ: Presbyterian and Reformed, 1991.

Pratt, Richard. "Historical Contingencies and Biblical Predictions." In *The Way of Wisdom*, edited by J. I. Packer and Sven K. Sonderlund, 180–203. Grand Rapids: Zondervan, 2000. This article can also be accessed at thirdmill.org.

Reymond, Robert L. *Jesus Divine Messiah*. Ross-shire, UK: Christian Focus, 2003.

Ridderbos, Herman N. *The Coming of the Kingdom*. Philadelphia: Presbyterian and Reformed, 1962.

Rydelnik, Michael. *The Messianic Hope: Is the Hebrew Bible Really Messianic?* Nashville: B&H Academic, 2010.

Sherman, Robert. *King, Priest, and Prophet: A Trinitarian Theology of Atonement*. New York: T&T Clark, 2004.

Sittema, John R. *Meeting Jesus at the Feast: Israel's Festivals and the Gospel.* Grandville, MI: Reformation Fellowship, 2010.

———. *With a Shepherd's Heart: Reclaiming the Pastoral Office of Elder.* Grandville, MI: Reformed Fellowship, 1996.

Sklar, Jay. *Sin, Impurity, Sacrifice, Atonement: The Priestly Conceptions.* Sheffield, UK: Sheffield Phoenix Press, 2005.

Stark, Rodney. *For the Glory of God.* Princeton, NJ: Princeton University Press, 2003.

Strauch, Alexander. *Biblical Eldership.* Rev. ed. Littleton, CO: Lewis and Roth, 1995.

Stroup, George W., III. "The Relevance of the *Minus Triplex* for Reformed Theology and Ministry." *Austin Seminary Bulletin* 98 (1983): 22–32.

Torrance, T. F. *Royal Priesthood: A Theology of Ordained Ministry.* 2nd ed. Edinburgh: T&T Clark, 1993.

Traeger, Sebastian, and Greg Gilbert. *The Gospel at Work: How Working for King Jesus Gives Purpose and Meaning to Our Jobs.* Grand Rapids: Zondervan, 2013.

Van Dam, Cornelius. *The Elder: Today's Ministry Rooted in All of Scripture.* Phillipsburg, NJ: P&R Publishing, 2009.

———. *The Urim and Thummim: A Means of Revelation in Ancient Israel.* Winona Lake, IN: Eisenbrauns, 1997.

VanGemeren, Willem A. *Interpreting the Prophetic Word.* Grand Rapids: Academie Books, 1990.

———, ed. *New International Dictionary of Old Testament Theology and Exegesis.* 5 vols. Grand Rapids: Zondervan, 1997.

Van Groningen, Gerard. *Messianic Revelation in the Old Testament.* Grand Rapids: Baker, 1990.

Vanhoye, Albert. *Old Testament Priests and the New Priest.* Petersham, MA: St. Bede's Publications, 1986.

Veith, Gene Edward, Jr. *God at Work: Your Christian Vocation in All of Life.* Wheaton, IL: Crossway, 2002.

Veith, Gene Edward, Jr., and Mary J. Moerbe. *Family Vocation: God's Calling in Marriage, Parenting, and Childhood.* Wheaton, IL: Crossway, 2012.

Vos, Geerhardus. *Biblical Theology*. Grand Rapids: Eerdmans, 1948.

———. *The Kingdom of God and the Church*. Nutley, NJ: Presbyterian and Reformed, 1972.

Wainwright, Geoffrey. *For Our Salvation: Two Approaches to the Work of Christ*. Grand Rapids: Eerdmans, 1997.

Waldron, Samuel E. *To Be Continued: Are Miraculous Gifts for Today?* Merrick, NY: Calvary Press, 2005.

Waltke, Bruce K. *Finding the Will of God: A Pagan Notion?* Grand Rapids: Eerdmans, 1995.

Waters, Guy. *How Jesus Runs the Church*. Phillipsburg, NJ: P&R Publishing, 2011.

Wenham, Gordon J. "Were David's Sons Priests?" *ZAW* 87 (1975): 79–82.

Wood, Leon J. *The Holy Spirit in the Old Testament*. Eugene, OR: Wipf and Stock, 1998.

Young, Edward J. *My Servants the Prophets*. Grand Rapids: Eerdmans, 1952.

Index of Scripture

Index of Subjects and Names

church discipline, 176
Clements, Ronald E., 41
Clowney, Edmund P., 94, 100, 163
Cole, R. Dennis, 71–72, 74, 108
consecration, 67, 70–72, 81–82,
    85–87, 89, 103, 134
covenant blessings and cursings, 11,
    22, 25–27, 36, 124
Craigie, Peter C., 24, 113
Crump, David, 50–51, 95
Currid, John D., 18, 20, 53, 65–66,
    69, 81–82, 107, 109–10

David, 2, 8, 27–28, 32, 35, 50, 61, 65,
    74–75, 91–92, 95, 99, 107–8,
    110, 120–39, 145, 147, 151–55,
    163, 166, 173
Davidic covenant, 32, 122–23, 126,
    128, 130, 135, 138
Davies, John, A., 124
Delitzsch, F., 116–17, 133–34, 136
Dennison, Charles, 170
de Vaux, Roland, 136
divination, 18–19, 27, 40
Durham, John I., 14

Ebert, Daniel J., IV, 166
Eden, 8–9, 59, 73, 178
Edgar, Thomas R., 163
elders, 40, 51, 119, 146, 164, 168–70,
    173, 175, 178, 180
Eleazar, 67, 73
Eli, 31, 118, 136
Elijah, 29, 34–36, 40, 42–44, 53–54,
    57, 92, 173
Elisha, 29, 34–36, 40, 54, 57

Eve, 5, 7–13, 15–17, 47, 59, 63–64, 105,
    157, 165, 178
exile, 15, 25–27, 109, 125, 130, 175
Ezekiel, 9, 19, 27–29, 37, 79, 150

Forster, Greg, 177
Frame, John M., 3, 86
Freeman, Hobart, 34–35
Fretheim, Terence E., 14

Gad, 32
garden of Gethsemane, 50, 89
Garrett, Duane A., 75, 162
Geivett, R. Douglas, 163
Geldenhuys, Norva, 54, 154
Gentry, Peter J., 10
George, Timothy, 86, 146, 148, 155,
    167, 172–73
Gershon, Kohath, and Merari, 72
Gilbert, Greg, 174
Goldingay, John, 30
Gordon, Robert P., 28
gospel, xiv, 143, 155, 158–59, 161, 164,
    167, 172, 174
Groningen, Gerard Van, 133, 135,
    185
Grudem, Wayne, 3, 163, 168

Habakkuk, 26, 51
Hamilton, Victor P., 106
Haran, Menahem, 64, 75
Harris, R. Laird, xv
Hartley, John E., 4
Hays, Richard B., 170
Heidelberg Catechism, 2, 166–67,
    171, 176

Hendriksen, William, 48, 51, 53, 87, 90, 98, 102, 142, 154
Hengstenberg, E. W., 46
Hertz, Karl H., 168
Hess, Richard S., 144, 151
Hezekiah, 126
high priest, 27, 52, 60, 62–68, 77–78, 80–84, 96, 110, 134, 171
Hilber, John W., 164
Hodge, Charles, 2, 164, 171
Hoeksema, Herman, 2
Hooykaas, R., 177
Horton, Michael, 3, 94
House, Paul R., 127, 136
Huffmon, Herbert B., 25
Hughes, Philip E., 96–98, 101, 157, 170, 173

image of God, 6, 105
intercession, 3, 38–39, 50, 95, 100–101
Isaac, 30, 107
Isaiah, 15, 28, 36, 39, 44, 49, 63, 83, 88–89, 100, 128–29, 142, 154, 161
Ithamar, 67

Jacob, 27, 30, 37, 64, 70, 107–8
Jehu, 35, 92
Jeon, Yong Ho, 125
Jeremiah, 3, 23, 26, 28, 37–39, 51–52, 79, 95, 99, 109, 129
Jeremias, Joachin, 50
Jeroboam, 33, 125–26
Jerusalem, 19, 23, 26, 37–38, 41, 49, 52–53, 74, 86, 89–90, 94, 96,
100, 122, 124–27, 132, 134, 144, 150, 154, 163, 169
Job, 3–4, 27, 59
Joel, 3, 39, 43, 160–63
Johnston, Gordon H., 135
John the Baptist, 36, 41–45, 54, 57, 89, 142, 146, 161
Jones, Mark, 166
Joshua, 27, 28, 30, 96, 109, 112, 115, 119
Josiah, 126

Kaiser, Walter C. Jr., 14, 61, 63, 65–66, 71
Kidner, Derek, 177
king
    believer as, 176
    Christ as, 1, 164
    Davidic, 85, 108, 123, 130, 134–35
    role of, 12–14, 16, 88, 105, 107–9, 111, 134, 144, 147, 158, 160, 165, 167–68, 175–76, 178–80
kingdom of God, 54, 143–46, 148–49, 176, 178
kingly ministry of the church, 175
Kinneer, Jack Dennis, 170
Kistemaker, Simon J., 98–99, 102, 157
Kline, Meredith, 12, 26, 109
Kruger, Michael J., xiii, 56, 162

Ladd, George Eldon, 146, 148
Lambert, W. G., 110
Lane, William L., 52, 154
Lazarus, 142–43
Leprohon, Ronald J., 110